Grammar Workshop

Level Orange

Beverly Ann Chin, Ph.D.
Senior Series Consultant
Professor of English
University of Montana
Missoula, MT

Sadlier

Grammar Workshop

Reviewers

The publisher wishes to thank the following teachers for their thorough review and thoughtful comments on portions of the series prior to publication.

Timothy Beaumont
Maplewood, New Jersey

Renea Boles
Flourtown, Pennsylvania

Stacy Donaghy
Little Rock, Arkansas

Christine Ganey
New York, New York

Maria James
San José, California

Stephanie Richardson
Compton, California

Nancy Wahl
New York, New York

Roseanne Williby
Omaha, Nebraska

Photo Credits

age fotostock/Andre Seale: 80. Alamy/Ablestock: 218; Bill Brooks: 113; CuboImages srl/Pasicc: 61; D. Hurst: 17 *left*; image100: 60; Wm. Baker/GhostWorks Images: 198. The American Library Association: 34. Animals Animals/Earth Scenes/Michael Fogden: 117. AP Photo/Pablo Martinez Monsivais: 170. Corbis/Bettmann: 16, 94; Jim Erickson: 172; Ocean: 180. Dreamstime/Starper: 82. Getty Images/AFP: 62; Dorling Kindersley/Steve Lyne: 89; Iconica/Diehm: 8; Iconica/Guy Bubb: 184; Iconica/Simon Wilkinson: 112; Lifesize/Mike Powell: 140; Photodisc: 70, 130; Photographer's Choice/PattiMcConville: 40; Stockbyte: 77; Stone/photo & co: 128; Stone/S Purdy Matthews: 125; Stone+/Tim Flach: 45; Taxi/Tony Anderson: 46; The Image Bank/Gary Vestal: 24. Incorporated Research Institute for Seismology/www.iris.edu: 192. iStockphoto.com/engineer89: 90; kycstudio: 17 *center*. Levi Strauss & Co. Archives: 17 *right*. Masterfile/Jeremy Woodhouse: 20. Punchstock/Digital Vision: 76, 88, 120, 124, 126; National Geographic: 169; Photodisc: 10, 48, 64, 152, 163, 194; Photographer's Choice RF: 209; Stockbyte: 208. Used under permission from Shutterstock.com/Dario Sabljak: 217; David Dea: 22; David MacFarlane: 53; Enrique Sallent: 171; Glenda M. Powers: 144; iofoto: 118; Ivanou Allaksandr: 86; Johanna Goodyear: 155; LaurensT: 30; Lisa C. McDonald: 176; mundoview: 28; Otna Ydur: 229; Peder Digre: 160; PHB.cz (Richard Semik): 31; Poznyakov: 230; Roland Loeffler: 196; Stephen Aaron Rees: 216; Tina Rencelj: 177; William Yuey: 168. Superstock/age fotostock: 81, 114, 228; Creatas: 84; Peter Barritt: 92. Thinkstock/Fuse: 183; Jupiterimages: 182. www.goodtimestove.com: 13.

Illustrators

Ron Berg: 18, 32, 65, 66, 72, 73, 164, 165, 167, 220, 223. Ken Bowser: 11, 42, 68, 69, 95, 132, 134, 135, 143, 212, 213, 214. John Ceballos: 49, 50, 100, 101, 102, 210. Mena Dolobowsky: 78, 145, 147. CD Hullinger: 104, 106, 148, 150, 178, 200, 201, 202. Nathan Jarvis: 12. Martin Lemelman: 96, 98, 99, 185, 186, 204, 206. Zina Saunders: 26, 116, 119, 122. Sam Ward: 44. Paul Weiner: 136, 138, 139, 224, 225, 227.

For additional online resources, go to grammarworkshop.com and enter the Student Access Code: GW13SGYK6BVN

Address inquiries to Permissions Department, William H. Sadlier, Inc., 9 Pine Street, New York, New York 10005-4700.

S® is a registered trademark of William H. Sadlier, Inc.

Printed in the United States of America.

ISBN: 978-1-4217-1054-9
7 8 9 RRDH 19 18 17

CONTENTS

Note to Students . . . 7

UNIT 1 SENTENCES

Lesson 1 Kinds of Sentences • *Write Your Own* . . . 8

Lesson 2 Complete Subjects and Predicates • *Write Your Own* . . . 12

Lesson 3 Simple Subjects • *Combining Sentences* . . . 16

Lesson 4 Simple Predicates • *Combining Sentences* . . . 20

Lesson 5 Compound Sentences • *Combining Sentences* . . . 24

Lesson 6 Complex Sentences • *Write Your Own* . . . 28

Lesson 7 Correcting Fragments and Run-ons • *Revising Sentences* . . . 32

Unit 1 Review . . . 36

Unit 1 Test . . . 38

UNIT 2 NOUNS

Lesson 8 Common and Proper Nouns • *Revising Sentences* . . . 40

Lesson 9 Singular and Plural Nouns • *Combining Sentences* . . . 44

Lesson 10 Irregular Plural Nouns • *Write Your Own* . . . 48

Lesson 11 Possessive Nouns • *Write Your Own* . . . 52

Unit 2 Review . . . 56

Unit 2 Test . . . 58

UNIT 3 Verbs

Lesson 12 Action Verbs • *Write Your Own* 60

Lesson 13 Present-Tense Verbs • *Revising Sentences* 64

Lesson 14 More Present-Tense Verbs • *Combining Sentences* 68

Lesson 15 Past-Tense Verbs • *Revising Sentences* 72

Lesson 16 Future-Tense Verbs • *Write Your Own* 76

Lesson 17 Linking Verbs • *Write Your Own* 80

Lesson 18 Main Verbs and Helping Verbs • *Write Your Own* 84

Lesson 19 Using Helping Verbs • *Write Your Own* 88

Lesson 20 Progressive Forms of Verbs • *Write Your Own* 92

Lesson 21 Irregular Verbs • *Write Your Own* 96

Lesson 22 More Irregular Verbs • *Write Your Own* 100

Lesson 23 Contractions with *Not* • *Revising Sentences* 104

Unit 3 Review 108

Unit 3 Test 110

UNIT 4 Adjectives, Adverbs, and Prepositions

Lesson 24 Adjectives • *Combining Sentences* 112

Lesson 25 *A, An, The* • *Revising Sentences* 116

Lesson 26 Demonstrative Adjectives • *Write Your Own* 120

Lesson 27 Comparing with Adjectives • *Write Your Own* 124

Lesson 28 Comparing with *More* and *Most* • *Write Your Own* 128

Lesson 29 Comparing with *Good* and *Bad* • *Write Your Own* 132

Lesson 30 Adverbs • *Revising Sentences* 136

Lesson 31 Comparing with Adverbs • *Write Your Own* 140

Lesson 32 Using *Good* and *Well* • *Write Your Own* 144

Lesson 33 Negatives • *Revising Sentences* 148

Lesson 34 Prepositions and Prepositional Phrases • *Revising Sentences* 152

Unit 4 Review 156

Unit 4 Test 158

UNIT 5 PRONOUNS

Lesson 35 Subject Pronouns • *Revising Sentences* 160

Lesson 36 Pronoun-Verb Agreement • *Write Your Own* 164

Lesson 37 Object Pronouns • *Revising Sentences* 168

Lesson 38 Using *I* and *Me* • *Combining Sentences* 172

Lesson 39 Possessive Pronouns • *Write Your Own* 176

Lesson 40 Relative Pronouns and Relative Adverbs • *Combining Sentences* 180

Lesson 41 Contractions with Pronouns • *Write Your Own* 184

Unit 5 Review 188

Unit 5 Test 190

UNIT 6 Capitalization, Punctuation, and Spelling

Lesson 42 Writing Sentences Correctly • *Revising Sentences* . . . 192

Lesson 43 Capitalizing Proper Nouns • *Write Your Own* . . . 196

Lesson 44 Abbreviations • *Write Your Own* . . . 200

Lesson 45 Titles • *Write Your Own* . . . 204

Lesson 46 Commas in a Series • *Combining Sentences* . . . 208

Lesson 47 More Commas • *Write Your Own* . . . 212

Lesson 48 Parts of a Letter • *Write Your Own* . . . 216

Lesson 49 Quotations • *Write Your Own* . . . 220

Lesson 50 Words Often Misspelled • *Write Your Own* . . . 224

Lesson 51 Words Often Confused • *Write Your Own* . . . 228

Unit 6 Review . . . 232

Unit 6 Test . . . 234

Index . . . 236

ONLINE COMPONENTS
available for computer and tablet at
grammarworkshop.com

(See page ii for the student access code.)

- Interactive Quiz for Every Lesson
- Extra Practice for Every Lesson
- Proofreading Worksheets for Every Unit

NOTE TO STUDENTS

You already know how to read, speak, and write English. So why should you learn grammar?

What Is Grammar?

Like all languages, English has rules about how words can be put together in sentences. Learning these rules will help you to speak and write so that everyone understands you. When you study grammar, you learn that words in English can be grouped into different parts. These parts include nouns, verbs, adjectives, adverbs, and pronouns. Grammar tells you how to put these parts together correctly.

How Will Grammar Help You?

Knowing grammar will help you to become a better reader, speaker, and writer. Knowing how language works will help you to read with more understanding. It will help you to express your feelings and ideas clearly. Your writing will be easier to follow. You will also make fewer mistakes when you do homework and take tests.

What Is Grammar Workshop?

Grammar Workshop is designed to teach you the rules of English and to give you lots and lots of practice. This book is called a WORKSHOP because it teaches in ways that make you work. You don't just read and memorize. You have to Learn, Practice, and Write.

Ready, Set, Go Grammar!

Now it's time to get started. Have fun, learn those rules—and go grammar!

Lesson 1: Kinds of Sentences

LEARN

A **sentence** is a group of words that expresses a complete thought.

- There are four kinds of sentences.

A **declarative sentence** makes a statement.
It ends with a period (**.**).

We watched a movie about volcanoes.

An **interrogative sentence** asks a question.
It ends with a question mark (**?**).

Have you ever seen a volcano?

An **imperative sentence** gives a command.
It ends with a period (**.**).

Stay away from active volcanoes.
Please be careful.

An **exclamatory sentence** shows strong feelings.
It ends with an exclamation mark (**!**).

How amazing that would be!
Wow, the colors are so bright!

- Every sentence begins with a capital letter and ends with a punctuation mark. The end punctuation you use depends on the kind of sentence you write.

PRACTICE

A *Read each sentence. Write **declarative, interrogative, imperative,** or **exclamatory** to tell what kind of sentence it is.*

1. What an incredible sight that is! ____________

2. Hot melted rock, gas, and steam burst from the volcano. ____________

3. Watch how the hot ash and lava flow down the mountain. ____________

4. What is lava? ____________________

5. Lava is hot liquid rock that comes out of a volcano. ____________________

6. Wow, a lava flow looks so dangerous! ____________________

7. Please leave the area immediately. ____________________

8. One famous volcano is Mount Vesuvius in Italy. ____________________

9. Will Mount Vesuvius erupt again? ____________________

10. I hope not! ____________________

B *Add the correct end punctuation to each sentence. Then write* ***declarative, interrogative, imperative,*** *or* ***exclamatory*** *to tell what kind of sentence it is.*

1. We learned more about volcanoes ____ ____________________

2. Wow, they can be so destructive ____ ____________________

3. Fortunately, they do not erupt very often ____ ____________________

4. What are the warning signs of an eruption ____ ____________________

5. One sign is a loud explosion ____ ____________________

6. Hey, that was such a loud clap ____ ____________________

7. You really scared me ____ ____________________

8. Move out of the path of the lava ____ ____________________

9. Look at the volcanic ash ____ ____________________

10. Please tell me more about volcanoes ____ ____________________

11. What else would you like to know ____ ____________________

12. Are there any volcanoes in our state ____ ____________________

C *Here is a conversation among some friends on a hike. The dialogue has three missing capital letters and seven missing or incorrect end marks. Look for the mistakes and correct them. Use the proofreading marks in the box.*

Remember

A **declarative sentence** makes a statement.
An **interrogative sentence** asks a question.
An **imperative sentence** gives a command.
An **exclamatory sentence** shows strong feelings.

Bianca Mount Rainier is the highest peak in the state of Washington.

Danny exactly how tall is it?

Bianca Read that sign over there

Maria Wow, it's 14,410 feet high

Bianca we'll only climb a thousand feet or so.

Maria What a relief that is

Danny Wait for me, you two.

Bianca Did you know that Mount Rainier is a volcano

Maria Are you serious.

Bianca the last major eruption was about 500 years ago.

Danny Will it erupt again soon!

Bianca The scientists say no

Maria Let's hurry up anyway.

Danny You can't be too careful!

Proofreading Marks

^	Add
⊙	Period
℘	Take out
≡	Capital letter
/	Small letter

Look Back Did you correct ten mistakes with capital letters and end marks?

Write Your Own

WRITE

Additional Resources at grammarworkshop.com

D *Imagine each situation below. Write a sentence that the person might say in the situation. Write the kind of sentence that is given in parentheses. The first one is done for you.*

Situation 1 Ms. Murray is teaching about volcanoes. She makes this statement about volcanoes. (declarative)

Ms. Murray *Hot ash or lava can erupt from a volcano.*

Situation 2 Your classmate Janet does not understand something about volcanoes. She raises her hand and asks a question. Write the question she asks. (interrogative)

Janet ______________________________

Situation 3 Lois is another classmate. She is very surprised by a fact she learns about volcanoes. Write the statement she makes to show her surprise. (exclamatory)

Lois ______________________________

Situation 4 Your friend Jerry hears that you have drawn some pictures of a volcano. He lets you know that he wants to look at them. Write the statement he makes. (imperative)

Jerry ______________________________

Situation 5 Luis thinks your drawings are really great. He wants to display them in some way. Write the question he asks. (interrogative)

Luis ______________________________

Proofreading Checklist ☑

- ❑ *Did you begin each sentence with a capital letter?*
- ❑ *Did you end each sentence with the correct end mark?*

Lesson 2: Complete Subjects and Predicates

LEARN

A **simple sentence** expresses a complete thought. It has a subject and a predicate.

- The **subject** tells *whom* or *what* the sentence is about.
  Maggie asks many questions.

The **predicate** tells what the subject *does* or *is*.
  Maggie **asks many questions**.

- The **complete subject** includes all the words in the subject part of the sentence. The **complete predicate** includes all the words in the predicate part of the sentence.

The complete subject or complete predicate can be one word or more than one word.

Complete Subject	Complete Predicate
Our little sister Maggie	smiles.
She	takes things apart.
My mom and dad	call her "the inventor."
All real inventors	are explorers.
The pictures in this book	gave us ideas.

PRACTICE

A *Read each sentence. Write* ***complete subject*** *or* ***complete predicate*** *to tell which part of the sentence is in* ***boldface****. The first one is done for you.*

1. **Benjamin Franklin** was a great inventor. complete subject
2. **His inventions** are part of our everyday lives. ____________
3. Ben **needed two pairs of eyeglasses**. ____________
4. One pair **was for reading**. ____________

PRACTICE A continued

5. **The other pair** was for seeing things at a distance. ____________________

6. **Franklin** hated carrying two pairs of glasses. ____________________

7. He **invented new glasses that solved the problem**. ____________________

8. **Ben** put half of a lens for distance on top. ____________________

9. He **put half of a lens for reading on the bottom**. ____________________

10. We **call these glasses "bifocals."** ____________________

B *Read each sentence. Draw a line between the complete subject and the complete predicate. Underline the complete subject once and the complete predicate twice. The first one is done for you.*

1. Ben Franklin | invented a new kind of stove.
2. The new stove got hot fast.
3. The new invention warmed every part of a room.
4. The Franklin stove was safer than a fire in a fireplace.
5. It burned less wood than other stoves.
6. People use Ben's stove even today.
7. Ben Franklin experimented with unusual ideas, too.
8. This busy scientist tested one idea in a pond.
9. Ben tied a kite to himself.
10. He swam in the pond.
11. The wind blew the kite.
12. The kite pulled Ben across the pond.

Franklin stove

C *Write a complete subject or a complete predicate to complete each sentence. Choose a subject or predicate from the box, or use a subject or predicate of your own. Write your sentence on the lines provided, adding the correct end punctuation.*

Remember

The **complete subject** tells *whom* or *what* the sentence is about.

The **complete predicate** tells what the subject *does* or *is*.

the gasoline engine	business and trade
turned nighttime into day	let people record information
early clocks	made travel much easier and safer
certain inventions	

1. have changed the world completely. ______________________________

____

2. The invention of writing ______________________________

____

3. grew quickly after the invention of money. ______________________________

____

4. The first maps ______________________________

____

5. helped people manage time better. ______________________________

____

6. made cars and trucks possible. ______________________________

____

7. The electric lightbulb ______________________________

____

Write Your Own

WRITE

Additional Resources at grammarworkshop.com

D *The computer is another invention that is changing our world. Use what you know about computers to complete each sentence. Add a complete subject or a complete predicate to each group of words. Write each sentence on the lines provided. Check a dictionary if you need help spelling a word.*

1. The invention of the computer ______________________________

____

2. use personal computers at home. ______________________________

____

3. Our school computers ______________________________

____

4. play games on computers. ______________________________

____

5. The computers in the library ______________________________

____

6. find information for reports and homework on the Internet. ______________

____

7. Modern cars, televisions, and music players ______________________

____

8. solve problems with computers. ______________________________

____

Proofreading Checklist ☑

- ❑ *Does each sentence begin with a capital letter?*
- ❑ *Does each sentence end with a period or other end mark?*
- ❑ *Does each sentence have a subject and a predicate?*

Lesson 3: Simple Subjects

LEARN

- The **simple subject** is the most important word in the complete subject. The simple subject tells exactly *whom* or *what* the subject is about.
- Sometimes the subject of a sentence is just one word. Sometimes it is a name. Then the simple subject and the complete subject are the same. Most of the time, however, the simple subject is part of the complete subject.

In the chart below, the simple subjects are shown in **boldface**.

Helen Keller sitting at a desk

Complete Subject	Complete Predicate
The school **librarian**	gave me a book.
The **book**	was about Helen Keller.
Helen Keller	lost her hearing and sight.
She	needed a special teacher.

PRACTICE

A *The complete subject in each sentence is in* **boldface**. *Circle the simple subject in the complete subject. Write it on the line.*

1. **This book** is about Helen Keller's remarkable life. ____________
2. **Helen Keller** became ill at the age of 19 months. ____________
3. **The mysterious illness** left her blind and deaf. ____________
4. **Anne Sullivan** was Helen's teacher. ____________
5. **The gifted teacher** taught Helen how to read and write. ____________
6. **Helen** graduated from college in 1904 with Anne's help. ____________
7. **The two women** traveled around the world. ____________

PRACTICE A *continued*

8. **The proud student** told people her story. ____________

9. **Large audiences** learned an important lesson from her. ____________

10. **An independent life** is possible even with physical challenges. ____________

B *Underline the complete subject in each sentence. Then circle the simple subject, and write it on the line.*

1. Levi Strauss made the first blue jeans in the 1870s. ____________
2. He was born in a part of Europe called Bavaria. ____________
3. This area is now a part of Germany. ____________
4. Strauss moved to New York in 1847. ____________
5. Levi joined the family clothing business. ____________
6. The young man brought the business to California. ____________
7. Many people searched for gold in California. ____________
8. The gold miners bought the pants Levi made. ____________
9. A heavy blue fabric made the pants strong. ____________
10. The family business expanded quickly. ____________
11. Many Americans wanted the waist overalls. ____________
12. "Waist overalls" was the old name for jeans. ____________

Remember

The **simple subject** is the most important word in the complete subject.

C *Write a complete subject to complete each sentence. Choose a complete subject from the box, or use a complete subject of your own. Then circle the simple subject.*

Most readers	Exciting historical events	
The person	A biography	Everyday events

_______________ tells the story of a person's life. _______________ might be an artist, an athlete, or a president. _______________ enjoy biographies very much. _______________ come alive in a well-written biography. _______________ can be interesting, too.

A biographer	These written records	
The actual writing	Most authors	Research

_______________ work very hard on biographies. _______________ is the first part of their job. _______________ must read old letters, diaries, and news stories about a person. _______________ reveal a great deal about the person. _______________ can take years and years.

Combining Sentences

WRITE

Additional Resources at grammarworkshop.com

Sometimes two related sentences have the same predicate.

Lena read a biography of Harriet Tubman.
Her friend read a biography of Harriet Tubman.

When this happens, you can combine the subjects and form one sentence. Use the word *and* to join the subjects. Combining the sentences in this way will make your writing smoother.

Lena **and** her friend read a biography of Harriet Tubman.

D *Each pair of sentences below has the same predicate. Combine the sentences by joining the subjects.*

1. Harriet Tubman lived in slavery. Her family lived in slavery. ____________________

____

2. Hardship shaped their lives. Struggles shaped their lives. ____________________

____

3. Harriet Tubman escaped. Her parents escaped. ____________________

____

4. Slave owners looked for Tubman. The police looked for Tubman. ____________________

____

5. Tubman never got caught. The slaves with her never got caught. ____________________

____

6. Careful planning led to her success. Quick thinking led to her success. ____________________

____

Look Back

Go back to the sentences you wrote. Underline the subjects you combined. Circle the word that joins them.

Lesson 4: Simple Predicates

LEARN

- The **simple predicate** is the most important word in the complete predicate. The simple predicate tells exactly what the subject *does* or *is*.
- Sometimes the predicate of a sentence is just one word. Then the simple predicate and the complete predicate are the same. Most of the time, however, the simple predicate is part of the complete predicate.

In the chart below, the simple predicates are shown in **boldface**.

Complete Subject	Complete Predicate
Everyone	**read**.
All of us	**searched** for information.
Our class	**planned** a trip to Ellis Island.
Ellis Island	**is** in New York City.
We	**rode** a ferryboat to the island.
Many tourists	**visit** the immigration museum.

PRACTICE

A *The complete predicate in each sentence is in* ***boldface****. Circle the simple predicate in the complete predicate. Write it on the line.*

1. This small island **is in New York Harbor.** ____________________
2. Samuel Ellis **owned the island at one time.** ____________________
3. The federal government **built a fort there in 1811.** ____________________
4. The fort **became an immigrant center in 1892.** ____________________
5. Immigrants **went there for inspections.** ____________________

6. The government **used the center for 62 years.** ____________________

7. Ellis Island **closed officially in November 1954.** ____________________

8. A new project **began in 1984.** ____________________

9. The Island **reopened as a museum.** ____________________

10. Over a million people **visit the museum each year.** ____________________

B *Underline the complete predicate in each sentence. Then circle the simple predicate, and write it on the line.*

1. Huge numbers of immigrants came to New York City. ____________________

2. About eight million entered the city from 1855 to 1890. ____________________

3. Many groups arrived at Ellis Island. ____________________

4. Most people left poor conditions back home. ____________________

5. The newcomers wanted better lives in America. ____________________

6. Some immigrants brought family members with them. ____________________

7. Others traveled by themselves. ____________________

8. Many immigrants crossed the ocean by steamship. ____________________

9. The ships docked at the piers. ____________________

10. Doctors examined the immigrants for illnesses. ____________________

11. Inspectors requested the proper papers. ____________________

12. Some passengers got special treatment. ____________________

13. Officials checked them aboard the ships. ____________________

14. The inspections lasted for hours. ____________________

15. Most immigrants passed inspection. ____________________

Remember The **simple predicate** is the most important word in the complete predicate.

C *Write a complete predicate to complete each sentence in this diary entry. Choose a complete predicate from the box, or use a complete predicate of your own. Then circle the simple predicate.*

asked us lots of questions
showed us our new home
cried with happiness
was over at last
carried us to my uncle's apartment
held her torch high above us
took us to Ellis Island

Dear Diary,

Today our ship steamed into New York Harbor. The beautiful Statue of Liberty ____________________. My mother and I ____________________. Our long voyage ____________________!

A small ferryboat ____________________. There the officials ____________________. Finally, we were free to go.

An underground train ____________________. He ____________________. Our new life in America is beginning at last!

Combining Sentences

WRITE

Additional Resources at grammarworkshop.com

Sometimes two related sentences have the same subject.

Mom studied history.
Mom shared what she knew.

When this happens, you can combine the predicates and form one sentence. Use the word *and* to join the predicates. Combining the sentences in this way will make your writing smoother.

Mom studied history **and** shared what she knew.

D *Each pair of sentences below has the same subject. Combine the sentences by joining the predicates.*

1. The United States changed. The United States grew. ____________________

____

2. Millions of immigrants left Europe. Millions of immigrants came here. __________

____

3. A father often came first. A father sent for his family later. ______________

____

4. The immigrants usually lived in big cities. The immigrants worked in jobs there.

____

____

5. New York City had the most immigrants. New York City became the largest city.

____

____

Look Back

Go back to the sentences you wrote. Underline the predicates you combined. Circle the word that joins them.

Lesson 5: Compound Sentences

LEARN

- A **simple sentence** has one subject and one predicate. It expresses one idea.
  The National Zoo is in Washington, D.C.

- Sometimes two simple sentences contain related ideas. You can combine these sentences to make a **compound sentence**. Use a connecting word such as *and*, *but*, or *or* to join the sentences.

  RELATED SENTENCES
  The National Zoo is huge. It has animals from all over the world.

  COMPOUND SENTENCE
  The National Zoo is huge, **and** it has animals from all over the world.

  RELATED SENTENCES
  Most zoos do not have pandas. The National Zoo does.

  COMPOUND SENTENCE
  Most zoos do not have pandas, **but** the National Zoo does.

  RELATED SENTENCES
  Would you like to go to the zoo? Would you rather see a movie?

  COMPOUND SENTENCE
  Would you like to go to the zoo, **or** would you rather see a movie?

The connecting words *and*, *but*, and *or* are called **coordinating conjunctions**. A comma (,) always goes before the conjunction in a compound sentence.

PRACTICE

A *Read each sentence. Write* **simple** *if the sentence is made up of only one idea. Write* **compound** *if the sentence is made up of two related ideas.*

1. Pandas feed mostly on bamboo plants. ______________

2. A panda's head is white, but its eyes and ears are black. ______________

3. Are pandas in the raccoon family, or are they true bears? ______________

4. Pandas are endangered, but people are working to protect them. ______

5. Grizzly bears walk slowly, but they can run fast. ______

6. Grizzlies eat many kinds of plants, and they eat fish, too. ______

7. A polar bear's coat is waterproof. ______

8. Polar bears are excellent swimmers. ______

9. Black bears are commonly found in the eastern United States. ______

10. Keep away from black bears, or you might get hurt. ______

B *Read each incomplete compound sentence. Underline the sentence below that best relates to it. Then combine the related sentences to form a compound sentence. Write the compound sentence on the line.*

1. Adult pandas weigh several hundred pounds, but ____.
   Pandas are in the bear family. Newborns weigh just one pound.

   ____

2. Brown bears eat meat, or ____.
   The tips of their hairs are white. They eat plants, insects, and fish.

   ____

3. Grizzly cubs can climb trees, but ____.
   Adult grizzlies cannot. They like honey.

   ____

4. Polar bears live near the water, and ____.
   They have small ears. They hunt seals there.

   ____

5. A brown bear has a shoulder hump, and ____.
   Grizzly bears are brown bears. It has very long claws.

   ____

C *One zoo posted this list of rules for visitors. The compound sentences on the list have six mistakes. Look for the mistakes and correct them. Use the proofreading marks in the box.*

Remember

A **simple sentence** has one subject and one predicate. It expresses one idea.

A **compound sentence** is formed by joining two simple sentences with a coordinating conjunction such as *and*, *but*, or *or*.

ZOO RULES

Enjoy your visit! Our zoo is a wonderful place to explore and these rules will keep you safe and happy.

- Please don't feed the animals. Our animals have special diets and human food can make them sick.
- Pets are not allowed at the zoo but guide dogs are permitted.
- Railings and fences protect you and they also keep our animals safe. Never extend fingers and arms through fences.
- Visitors may carry personal digital devices but they must use headphones. Noise can disturb both animals and people.
- Don't litter. Place all your trash in the bins or our zoo won't be a pleasant place to visit.

Proofreading Marks

∧	Add
⊙	Period
ℓ	Take out
≡	Capital letter
/	Small letter

Look Back Did you correct six mistakes in the compound sentences?

Combining Sentences

WRITE

Additional Resources at grammarworkshop.com

D *Each pair of sentences below contains related ideas. Combine the sentences to form a compound sentence. Use the coordinating conjunction in parentheses to join them. Remember to put a comma before the joining word. The first one is done for you.*

1. Zookeepers know more about how an animal lives. They build better zoos. (and)

Zookeepers know more about how an animal lives, and they build better zoos.

2. Animals move around freely. People can still get a good view of them. (but)

____

____

3. Conditions must be just right in a zoo. Animals get sick. (or) ____________

____

4. Polar bears need icy cold water. Lions need warm temperatures. (but) ____________

____

5. Zoo animals need to stay busy. They will become bored and unhappy. (or)

____

____

6. Apes search for their own food in today's zoos. Some zoo elephants even paint pictures. (and) ____________

____

7. The field feels as if it is the giraffes' natural home. There is lots of room to roam. (and) ____________

____

8. Modern zoos are difficult to build and run. They're worth it. (but) ____________

____

Lesson 6: Complex Sentences

LEARN

- You have learned about compound sentences. Compound sentences combine related ideas using a connecting word such as *and*, *but*, or *or*.

  A **complex sentence** also combines related ideas. The ideas are joined by a **subordinating conjunction**. Look at the sentence below.

  The canyon is wide **because** the river has eroded its walls.

  The subordinating conjunction *because* joins the two related ideas.

The following **subordinating conjunctions** are often used to connect related ideas.

Subordinating Conjunctions			
after	although	because	before
since	until	when	while

- The subordinating conjunction may come in the middle of the sentence.

  Plains are mostly flat **although** some have small hills.

- The subordinating conjunction may come at the beginning of the sentence.

  Although some have small hills, plains are mostly flat.

  Notice that when the first idea in the sentence begins with a subordinating conjunction, a comma follows that idea.

PRACTICE

A *Read each sentence. Write* **complex** *if the sentence is made up of two related ideas joined by a subordinating conjunction. Write* **not complex** *if it is not a complex sentence.*

1. After we made the last turn, we reached the mountain. ____________

2. We wanted to see the mountain because it is so majestic. ____________

3. A mountain is higher than the area around it. ____________

4. The taller mountains reach into the colder layers of the atmosphere. ____________________

5. Since the mountain slope is gentle, it is perfect for skiing. ____________________

6. Mountains take millions of years to form. ____________________

7. A mountain can form when Earth's crust bends. ____________________

8. Unlike mountains, the plains are low and flat. ____________________

9. Because they are low-lying areas, plains can flood easily. ____________________

10. Plains may be surrounded by small hills or mountains. ____________________

B *Read each complex sentence. Write the subordinating conjunction that joins the two related ideas. The first one is done for you.*

1. When an earthquake happens, you can take steps to be safe. When

2. You should take cover until the ground stops shaking. ____________________

3. Since earthquakes sometimes happen under the ocean, you may see waves on the surface. ____________________

4. A tsunami can take place after an earthquake strikes. ____________________

5. Some cities are prepared for an earthquake because they have had so many. ____________________

6. Although some earthquakes are dangerous, most are not. ____________________

7. Scientists could study an earthquake better when they had the latest tools. ____________________

8. Before an earthquake hits, some animals seem nervous. ____________________

9. We saw a wide crack in the ground while we were hiking. ____________________

10. The ground cracked because parts of the earth had split apart. ____________________

C *Write a subordinating conjunction to complete each sentence. Choose a subordinating conjunction from the box, or use a subordinating conjunction of your own.*

Remember A **complex sentence** is formed by joining two related ideas with a subordinating conjunction.

after	although	because	before
since	until	when	while

1. Thomas went to Costa Rica ________________ he wanted to see a volcano.

2. ________________ I have read about volcanoes, I haven't seen one.

3. Thomas showed us his photographs ________________ he returned from his trip.

4. ________________ she is a park ranger at Denali National Park, Aunt Mary can tell us about glaciers.

5. Glaciers leave rocks behind ________________ they move across the land.

6. ________________ we traveled to Alaska last spring, I had never seen a glacier.

7. I read books about glaciers ________________ we took our trip.

8. I saw one of these large sheets of ice

________________ our plane landed.

9. I put on a heavy coat ________________ it is cold on top of a glacier.

10. ________________ there once were many glaciers in America, there are few today.

11. ________________ some glaciers contain a lot of air, they can look blue.

12. We heard loud noises ________________ pieces of a glacier broke off.

Write Your Own

WRITE

Additional Resources at grammarworkshop.com

D *Imagine a beautiful island that you want people to visit. Use the items below to create a persuasive article about the island. Be sure to use complete sentences. Check a dictionary if you need help spelling a word.*

1. because the island is far away

____

____

2. after you arrive ______________________________

____

3. since so much water surrounds the island ______________________________

____

4. when you are at the beach ______________________________

____

5. although there is a volcano ______________________________

____

6. until you see the amazing flowers here ______________________________

____

7. while you are at the beach ______________________________

____

8. before you leave ______________________________

____

Proofreading Checklist ☑

- ❑ *Does each sentence use correct capitalization?*
- ❑ *Does each sentence that begins with a subordinating conjunction have a comma after the first idea?*

Lesson 7: Correcting Fragments and Run-ons

LEARN

- A **fragment** is an incomplete sentence. The subject or predicate might be missing. To correct this kind of fragment, add a subject or a predicate.

FRAGMENT Bought a children's book.

SENTENCE My sister bought a children's book.

Add a subject.

FRAGMENT The book.

SENTENCE The book is for my brother.

Add a predicate.

- A **run-on sentence** is two complete sentences that run together. One way to correct a run-on sentence is to make two separate sentences. Another way is to make a compound sentence.

RUN-ON

She likes to draw she wants to be an artist.

CORRECTED SENTENCE

She likes to draw. She wants to be an artist.

two separate sentences

CORRECTED SENTENCE

She likes to draw, and she wants to be an artist.

compound sentence

PRACTICE

A *Read each group of words. Circle **sentence, fragment,** or **run-on** to describe it.*

1. Lane Smith is an illustrator. *sentence* *fragment* *run-on*

2. The young artist. *sentence* *fragment* *run-on*

3. He loved to draw pictures he loved baseball. *sentence* *fragment* *run-on*

4. He is grateful to his teachers. *sentence* *fragment* *run-on*

5. They encouraged him they helped him. *sentence* *fragment* *run-on*

6. One of his teachers. *sentence* *fragment* *run-on*

7. Tried out different art supplies. *sentence* *fragment* *run-on*

8. This artist has a great imagination. *sentence* *fragment* *run-on*

B *Make each fragment a complete sentence by matching it with the correct subject or predicate. Write the letter of the words you choose on the line.*

____	**1.** *The Tale of Peter Rabbit*	**a.** is Beatrix Potter.
____	**2.** The author's name	**b.** is a well-known children's book.
____	**3.** wrote the story in a letter.	**c.** The letter
____	**4.** was for a little boy who was sick.	**d.** later turned the story into a book.
____	**5.** Potter	**e.** Beatrix

Write each run-on sentence as a compound sentence.

6. Beatrix Potter made the story longer she redrew the pictures, too. ____________

____

7. She wanted to make books for children she wanted to make them easy to hold.

____

8. Beatrix made the books little she used sturdy paper. ____________

____

Write each run-on sentence as two separate sentences.

9. Beatrix Potter grew up in England drawing was her favorite hobby.

____

10. Beatrix had a younger brother both children loved plants and animals.

____

C *Leah wrote this report. It contains three fragments and three run-on sentences. Use the proofreading marks in the box to correct the mistakes. Add a subject or predicate to correct each fragment. Write each run-on sentence as a compound sentence or as two separate sentences.*

Remember

A **fragment** is an incomplete sentence.

A **run-on sentence** is two complete sentences that run together.

Proofreading Marks

∧	Add
⊙	Period
℘	Take out
≡	Capital letter
/	Small letter

Thousands of children's books are published each year most of them have good illustrations. However, only one book gets the Caldecott Medal. Goes to the best illustrator of a children's book.

The Caldecott Medal is a very special honor. The American Library Association presents the award. Librarians study the year's new children's books, they vote on the best one.

The first Caldecott Medal was given in 1938. Since then, many great illustrators have won it. Encourages artists to draw fine pictures for young readers.

Sometimes, you might see a gold Caldecott Medal on a book. This medal. Take a minute to look inside it you're sure to find some outstanding illustrations.

Look Back Did you correct three fragments and three run-on sentences?

Revising Sentences

Additional Resources at grammarworkshop.com

WRITE

D *Add a subject or predicate to each fragment to make a complete sentence. Write the sentence on the line.*

1. A book's illustrations. ______________________________

____

2. Add interest to the story. ______________________________

____

3. Show the mood and feelings in a story, too. ______________________________

____

4. Drawings, paintings, and photographs. ______________________________

____

5. Photographs. ______________________________

____

6. My favorite book illustrator. ______________________________

____

7. The Caldecott Medal. ______________________________

____

8. Are fun to read. ______________________________

____

9. Books without illustrations. ______________________________

____

10. Are on display in the library. ______________________________

____

Unit 1 Review
Lessons 1–7

Kinds of Sentences (pp. 8–11) *Read each sentence. Write **declarative, interrogative, imperative,** or **exclamatory** to tell what kind of sentence it is.*

1. A tornado hit the town yesterday. ____________________

2. Did you see the tornado? ____________________

3. Look at these photos. ____________________

4. How lucky we were! ____________________

Complete Subjects and Predicates (pp. 12–15) *Read each sentence. Draw a line between the complete subject and the complete predicate. Underline the complete subject once and the complete predicate twice.*

5. A tornado looks like a dark funnel-shaped cloud.

6. Winds whirl around at high speeds.

7. These dangerous storms move in a narrow path across the earth.

8. The twisting cloud picks up dirt from the ground.

Simple Subjects (pp. 16–19) *Read each sentence. Underline the complete subject. Then circle the simple subject.*

9. About 700 tornadoes occur in the United States each year.

10. These powerful storms damage everything in their path.

11. The gusty winds uproot trees.

12. Some automobiles fly through the air for hundreds of feet.

Simple Predicates (pp. 20–23) *Read each sentence. Underline the complete predicate. Then circle the simple predicate.*

13. Most tornadoes hit the midwestern states.

14. Certain weather conditions produce these storms.

15. Weather scientists track tornadoes.

16. The scientists announce tornado warnings whenever possible.

Compound Sentences (pp. 24–27) *Read each sentence. Write **simple** if the sentence is made up of only one idea. Write **compound** if the sentence is made up of two related ideas.*

17. Most tornadoes occur on hot and humid days. ____________________

18. Warm air rises rapidly, and sometimes it begins to spin. ____________________

19. This spinning air sometimes forms a tornado. ____________________

20. The tornado can stay in the air, or it might touch down on the ground. ____________________

Complex Sentences (pp. 28–31) *Read each sentence. Write **complex** if it is a complex sentence. Write **not complex** if it is not a complex sentence.*

21. Although most tornadoes last only a few minutes, they can cause great damage. ____________________

22. The Fujita scale or F-scale measures a tornado's intensity. ____________________

23. An F5 rating on the F-scale stands for the greatest wind strength any tornado can have. ____________________

24. A tornado warning will be issued when radar spots powerful winds. ____________________

Correcting Fragments and Run-ons (pp. 32–35) *Read each group of words. Write **sentence, fragment,** or **run-on** to describe it.*

25. A storm cellar gives the best protection from a tornado a basement is the next safest place. ____________________

26. The National Weather Service. ____________________

27. Always keep away from windows during a tornado. ____________________

28. Warns people about tornadoes. ____________________

Unit 1 Test

DIRECTIONS *Fill in the circle next to the sentence that shows the correct use of capital letters and end punctuation. The first one is done for you.*

1.
- ○ Many foods come from all over the world
- ○ Did potatoes come from Peru.
- ○ chocolate was a favorite food in Mexico?
- ● How I love chocolate!

2.
- ○ Did peanuts first grow in North America!
- ○ Are they members of the pea family, or do they belong to a different group?
- ○ Spanish explorers brought peanuts to Europe?
- ○ Wow, peanuts really got around

3.
- ○ Native Americans grew corn, peppers, and squash
- ○ bananas are native to South America!
- ○ Are you sure about that?
- ○ I will know, after I read this encyclopedia article.

4.
- ○ Peppers are called chilies in Mexico
- ○ try a bite of this.
- ○ Wow, it's really hot?
- ○ I love hot peppers on pizza.

5.
- ○ Are the tomato and the potato related?
- ○ People once thought tomatoes were poisonous?
- ○ what a silly idea that is!
- ○ How did they make pizza without tomatoes.

6.
- ○ Pumpkins are American, too?
- ○ Wow, those pumpkins are heavy!
- ○ did Native Americans share pumpkins with early settlers?
- ○ When did people first carve jack-o'-lanterns

7.
- ○ turkey is another American food.
- ○ Was it the main dish at the first Thanksgiving.
- ○ The turkey almost became our national bird.
- ○ have you ever seen a wild turkey

8.
- ○ Explorers searched for new lands?
- ○ They often discovered new foods on their journeys
- ○ Tell me which American foods you like best.
- ○ our meals would be boring without such foods!

DIRECTIONS *Read the paragraphs, and look carefully at each underlined part. Fill in the circle next to the answer choice that shows the correct use of capital letters and end punctuation. If the underlined part is already correct, fill in the circle for "Correct as is." The first one is done for you.*

The high mountains of Peru are cold. The Incas could not grow corn there but they (9) could grow potatoes. How did those potatoes get to Europe! the (10) early Spanish explorers of Peru brought them to Spain in the 1530s. What a success potatoes were at first, wealthy people (11) had parties just to try the new food

Then some questions arose. Did potatoes cause disease, or did they (12) poison the soil? For a while, many Europeans believed potatoes were dangerous. Fortunately, people got over such a silly idea. They planted potatoes widely and soon the crop (13) was plentiful. How important the new crop turned out to be many Europeans (14) had enough food for the first time.

9.
- ● there, but they
- ○ there. but they
- ○ there, But they
- ○ Correct as is

10.
- ○ Europe the
- ○ Europe. The
- ○ Europe? The
- ○ Correct as is

11.
- ○ first, wealthy people
- ○ first! Wealthy people
- ○ first. Wealthy people
- ○ Correct as is

12.
- ○ disease or did they
- ○ disease? or did they
- ○ disease, Or did they
- ○ Correct as is

13.
- ○ widely, and soon the crop
- ○ widely, And soon the crop
- ○ widely. and soon the crop
- ○ Correct as is

14.
- ○ be. Many Europeans
- ○ be, many Europeans
- ○ be! Many Europeans
- ○ Correct as is

Lesson 8: Common and Proper Nouns

LEARN

- A **noun** is a word that names a person, place, or thing. A **common noun** names any person, place, or thing.
  The **girl** visited the **fountain** in the **park**.
- A **proper noun** names a specific person, place, or thing. It can be one word or more than one word.
  Julia visited **Bethesda Fountain** in **Central Park**.
- Each important word in a proper noun begins with a capital letter.

	Common	Proper
Person	teacher	Ms. Jones
Place	city	Los Angeles
Thing	statue	Statue of Liberty

Bethesda Fountain in Central Park

- Ideas such as *fear* and *greed* are called **abstract nouns**. You can't see or touch them, but they are still nouns. Abstract nouns are always common nouns.
  Greed was his undoing.

PRACTICE

A *Match each common noun with a proper noun. Write the letter of the proper noun on the line.*

Common Nouns	Proper Nouns
_____ **1.** month	**a.** Mexico
_____ **2.** country	**b.** October

____ **3.** holiday		**c.** Venus
____ **4.** planet		**d.** Fourth of July
____ **5.** building		**e.** White House
____ **6.** state		**f.** Asia
____ **7.** continent		**g.** Abraham Lincoln
____ **8.** day of the week		**h.** Nebraska
____ **9.** lake		**i.** Monday
____ **10.** president		**j.** Lake Charles

B *Read each sentence. Write* ***common*** *if the noun in* ***boldface*** *is a common noun. Write* ***proper*** *if it is a proper noun.*

1. Dora visited **Yellowstone National Park** last summer. ____________

2. The **park** lies mainly in Wyoming. ____________

3. Is it the largest national park in the **United States**? ____________

4. The park's geysers attract many **visitors**. ____________

5. Water from inside the earth shoots out of a **geyser**. ____________

6. **Old Faithful** is the most famous geyser. ____________

7. Spectators feel great **excitement** when this geyser erupts. ____________

8. People visit the **Mammoth Hot Springs**, too. ____________

9. **Dora** hiked up to Yellowstone Lake. ____________

10. Her **love** of Yellowstone is apparent. ____________

C *Dora wrote this letter to her grandmother. She made twelve mistakes when writing common and proper nouns. Look for the mistakes and fix them. Use the proofreading marks in the box.*

Remember

Each important word in a proper noun begins with a capital letter.

Proofreading Marks

- ^ Add
- ⊙ Period
- ℓ Take out
- ≡ Capital letter
- / Small letter

Dear Grandma,

Can you imagine a Canyon 18 miles wide and a mile deep? Well, if you were here in Grand Canyon national Park in arizona, you wouldn't have to. You could be hiking in it with us!

The Trip is not all hiking, though. On tuesday, we rafted down the Colorado river for about 10 Miles! We only got wet twice, and we got to see some Sheep. We might take a mule Trip tomorrow to a place called Phantom ranch. That sounds scary, but I still want to go.

We will be home by september 1st, and I will see you at our picnic on Labor day. I can't wait to tell you more about the trip!

Love,

Dora

Look Back Did you correct twelve mistakes?

Revising Sentences

WRITE

Additional Resources at grammarworkshop.com

Sometimes your sentences might have nouns that are not clear or specific.

Our train travels along the **river**.
We can see **boats** on the water.

You can replace these nouns with nouns that are more descriptive. The words you choose can be either common or proper nouns.

Our train travels along the **Hudson River**.
We can see **sailboats** on the water.

D *In each sentence below, change the word or words in **boldface** to a more descriptive noun. Use either a common noun or a proper noun. Write the new sentence on the line.*

1. I would like to visit **a city** some day.

____

2. There is a really famous **thing** there.

____

3. I will probably invite **a friend** to go with me.

____

4. We could pack **food** for lunch.

____

5. We will bring some **fruit** for snacktime, too.

____

6. We would send postcards to **a teacher**.

____

7. During the trip home, we would play **a game**.

____

Look Back

Go back to the sentences you wrote.
Circle the more descriptive nouns you used.

Lesson 9: Singular and Plural Nouns

LEARN

- Nouns can be singular or plural. A **singular noun** names one person, place, or thing. A **plural noun** names more than one person, place, or thing.

SINGULAR	I visited an **exhibit** at the county fair.
PLURAL	I visited three **exhibits** at the county fair.

- Follow these rules to make plural nouns.
  - Add *-s* to most singular nouns.

SINGULAR	bird	bee	flower	vegetable
PLURAL	bird**s**	bee**s**	flower**s**	vegetable**s**

  - Add *-es* when a singular noun ends in *s, ss, ch, sh,* or *x*.

SINGULAR	bus	dress	porch	dish	ax
PLURAL	bus**es**	dress**es**	porch**es**	dish**es**	ax**es**

  - When a singular noun ends in a vowel and *y*, add *-s*.

SINGULAR	boy	key	holiday
PLURAL	boy**s**	key**s**	holiday**s**

  - When a singular noun ends in a consonant and *y*, change the *y* to *i*, and add *-es*.

SINGULAR	lady	family	cherry
PLURAL	lad**ies**	famil**ies**	cherr**ies**

PRACTICE

A *Write the plural form of each noun.*

1. wish ____________________
2. bunny ____________________
3. patch ____________________
4. donkey ____________________
5. tax ____________________
6. celebration ____________________
7. guess ____________________
8. song ____________________
9. party ____________________
10. fox ____________________

B *Write the plural form of the noun in parentheses to complete each sentence.*

1. Many ____________________ in our state hold fairs each summer. (county)
2. Different farm ____________________ help pay for the events. (group)
3. Tourists arrive in cars and ____________________. (bus)
4. The ____________________ at the fair are always interesting. (event)
5. Some ____________________ sell products to the visitors. (business)
6. ________________ of prize-winning fruits and vegetables fill one building. (box)
7. The apples and ____________________ always look delicious. (peach)
8. You can sample the homemade jams and ____________________. (jelly)
9. ____________________ of fresh-squeezed juice are on sale, too. (glass)
10. ____________________ made with local cheeses are popular. (sandwich)
11. Most children and ____________________ love the animal exhibits. (baby)
12. Horses and ____________________ fill one huge barn. (pony)
13. Visitors look at the colorful chickens and ____________________. (turkey)
14. The best cows and sheep win blue ribbons for ____________________. (prize)
15. We look forward to the fair for ____________________. (month)

C *Ron wrote this report. He made nine mistakes when writing nouns. Sometimes he misspelled plural nouns. At other times, he used a plural noun for a singular noun or a singular noun for a plural noun. Use the proofreading marks to correct these mistakes.*

Remember

If a noun ends in *s, ss, ch, sh,* or *x*, add -es to form the plural.

If a noun ends in a consonant and *y*, change the *y* to *i*, and add *-es* to form the plural.

Proofreading Marks

^	Add
⊙	Period
ℯ/	Take out
≡	Capital letter
/	Small letter

Many communitys today celebrate *Cinco de Mayo*. These words are Spanish for the "Fifth of May." On May 5, 1862, the Mexican army defeated a much larger French army. The Mexican people were proud of this important victory, and the day became a holidays.

Cinco de Mayo celebrates Mexican history and culture. In some large city, official organize a big fiesta, or festival. In Los Angeles, almost a million residents attend. Boy and girls in colorful costumees perform folk dances. Bands play traditional music. Different business prepare Mexican dishs for the crowd. Parades are also usually part of the big day.

Cinco de Mayo is a great way for familys and neighbors to remember their heritage and have fun, too!

Look Back **Did you correct nine mistakes with nouns?**

Combining Sentences

WRITE

Additional Resources at grammarworkshop.com

Singular and plural nouns can appear in the subject or the predicate of a sentence. Sometimes you can combine two related sentences by joining the nouns. Use the conjunction *and* or *or* to join the nouns.

Cowboys ride in the rodeo.
Cowgirls ride in the rodeo.
Cowboys **and** cowgirls ride in the rodeo.

The rodeo will take place in the United States.
The rodeo will take place in Canada.
The rodeo will take place in the United States **or** Canada.

D *Combine each pair of sentences by joining nouns in the subject or predicate. Use the conjunction in parentheses to join the nouns.*

1. Rodeo is based on traditions from the United States. Rodeo is based on traditions from Mexico. (and) ______________________

____

2. The events developed from chores on ranches. The events developed from activities on ranches. (and) ______________________

____

3. Rodeo riders enter contests. Rodeo riders enter races. (or) ______________________

____

4. The cowboys might perform first. The cowgirls might perform first. (or) ______________________

____

5. Audiences enjoy the action. Audiences enjoy the excitement. (and) ______________________

____

Look Back

Look back at the sentences you wrote. Underline the nouns you joined in the subject or predicate.

Lesson 10: Irregular Plural Nouns

LEARN

- Some nouns have **irregular plurals**. In most cases, the spelling of the singular noun changes to form the plural.

SINGULAR	man	woman	child	tooth
PLURAL	men	women	children	teeth
SINGULAR	foot	goose	mouse	ox
PLURAL	feet	geese	mice	oxen

- In a few cases, the plural noun and the singular noun are the same.

SINGULAR	One **deer** nibbles the grass.
PLURAL	Three **deer** stand and watch.
SINGULAR	This **sheep** is white.
PLURAL	The other two **sheep** are brown.
SINGULAR	A **moose** swam across the lake.
PLURAL	Several **moose** live on the island.

PRACTICE

A *Read each sentence. Write **singular** if the noun in **boldface** is a singular noun. Write **plural** if it is a plural noun.*

1. The **children** in our class went to the wildlife refuge. ____________
2. A friendly **man** met us at the entrance. ____________
3. Several Canada **geese** were swimming in the pond. ____________
4. A single **moose** stood at the water's edge. ____________
5. We were as quiet as **mice**, but it still ran away. ____________
6. Two **women** showed us a tree cut down by a beaver. ____________
7. What sharp **teeth** that beaver must have! ____________
8. At sunset, a **deer** came down to the water to drink. ____________

9. Three other **deer** soon followed. ____________________

10. An **ox** stood alone in the field. ____________________

B *Write the plural form of the noun in parentheses to complete each sentence.*

1. Twelve ____________________ are honking in the sky above. (goose)

2. Three ____________________ look up at the big birds. (woman)

3. A group of ____________________ is eating from a bush. (deer)

4. The animals use their ____________________ to tear the leaves. (tooth)

5. Several ____________________ chewed the bark from this young tree. (mouse)

6. Many tiny ____________________ left prints in the mud. (foot)

7. The four ____________________ point with excitement across the lake. (child)

8. Two huge ____________________ are standing on the other side. (moose)

9. At a farm museum, two ____________________ tell us about the past. (man)

10. Two ____________________ pull a plow in a field. (ox)

11. A flock of ____________________ grazes in a meadow nearby. (sheep)

12. A family of ____________________ races across the field. (mouse)

C *Connie wrote this poem about the first day of spring. She made six mistakes when forming irregular plural nouns. Look for the mistakes, and fix them. Use the proofreading marks in the box.*

Remember
For most **irregular plurals**, the spelling of the singular noun changes to form the plural.

Proofreading Marks

^	Add
⊙	Period
℘	Take out
≡	Capital letter
/	Small letter

The First Day of Spring

The first day of spring can't be beat!
I smile at all the people I meet.
The other childs are smiling, too.
We all go together to the zoo.

The reindeers and lions are having fun.
They all seem glad that winter is done.
The bighorn sheeps don't say, "Baa," today.
Instead, they're yelling, "Hip, Hip, Hooray!"

Up in the sky, six gooses are squawking.
It almost sounds as if they're talking
About spring to the mans and womens below,
But what they're saying, we'll never know.

Look Back Did you correct six irregular plural nouns?

Write Your Own

WRITE

Additional Resources at grammarworkshop.com

D *Read these rhymes about irregular plural nouns. Then write three rhymes of your own. Use the words in parentheses in your rhymes.*

One bird is a goose,
And two are called geese.
But the plural of moose
Can never be meese!

The singular is man,
The plural is men.
But the plural of pan
Just cannot be pen!

1. ______________________________ (foot)

______________________________ (feet)

______________________________ (boot)

______________________________ (beet)

2. ______________________________ (ox)

______________________________ (oxen)

______________________________ (fox)

______________________________ (foxen)

3. ______________________________ (mouse)

______________________________ (mice)

______________________________ (blouse)

______________________________ (blice)

Proofreading Checklist ☑

- ❏ *Did you use the words in parentheses in your rhymes?*
- ❏ *Did you spell the real singular and plural nouns correctly?*

Lesson 11: Possessive Nouns

LEARN

A **possessive noun** is a noun that shows who or what has something.

Janet's mother teaches quilting.
She displayed the **students'** quilts.

Both singular and plural nouns can be made possessive.

- To make a singular noun possessive, add an apostrophe and *-s*.

SINGULAR	Janet	family	class
SINGULAR POSSESSIVE	Janet**'s**	family**'s**	class**'s**

- To make a plural noun that ends in *-s* possessive, add only an apostrophe.

PLURAL	students	families	classes
PLURAL POSSESSIVE	students'	families'	classes'

- To make a plural noun that does not end in *-s* possessive, add an apostrophe and *-s*.

PLURAL	women	children	sheep
PLURAL POSSESSIVE	women**'s**	children**'s**	sheep**'s**

PRACTICE

A *Write the possessive form of the noun in* ***boldface***.

1. the tools owned by the **workers** — the ______________ tools
2. the hats belonging to the **men** — the ______________ hats
3. the rugs belonging to the **museum** — the ______________ rugs
4. the sizes of the **frames** — the ______________ sizes
5. the clay belonging to the **potter** — the ______________ clay
6. the quilt owned by **Mia** — ______________ quilt

7. the smocks used by the **painters** the ____________ smocks

8. the purchases of the **tourists** the ____________ purchases

9. the design of the **building** the ____________ design

10. the collection owned by **Gus** ____________ collection

B *Write the possessive form of the noun in parentheses that correctly completes each sentence.*

1. Our ____________ first craft fair was a great success. (town)

2. Our ____________ projects were on display. (neighbors)

3. Some ____________ embroidered pillows were in the show. (women)

4. ____________ hand-carved chairs attracted a crowd. (Mr. Moss)

5. His birdhouses attracted the ____________ attention. (children)

6. ____________ aunt is a weaver. (Sharon)

7. She uses wool from a local ____________ sheep. (farmer)

8. The ____________ wool is soft. (sheep)

9. A ____________ wheel turned slowly in one area. (potter)

10. A ____________ hands slowly shaped clay into a vase. (man)

11. The ____________ shape was almost perfect! (vase)

12. All the artists answered ____________ questions. (visitors)

Remember

A **possessive noun** shows who or what owns or has something.

C *David wrote about a class trip to a glassblower's workshop. He made seven mistakes when writing possessive nouns. Look for the mistakes, and fix them. Use the proofreading marks in the box.*

Our classs visit to Ms. Andersons' glass workshop was really interesting. I especially enjoyed the glassblowing demonstration. It gave everyone a firsthand look at this artists' amazing skills.

The workshops furnace heated some glass until it melted. When the mixtures temperature was about 2000°F, Ms. Anderson briefly dipped a hollow iron blowpipe into it. A small amount of melted glass stuck to the blowpipes tip.

Ms. Anderson then blew gently into the blowpipe. Her breath forced the glass to bulge out and form a hollow bulb. With a few twists and turns, the glass'es final shape appeared. It was now a beautiful vase.

Of all the crafts I have seen so far, handmade glass fascinates me the most.

Proofreading Marks

^	Add
⊙	Period
ℓ/	Take out
≡	Capital letter
/	Small letter

Look Back Did you correct seven possessive nouns?

Write Your Own

WRITE

Additional Resources at grammarworkshop.com

D *Rewrite each phrase using a possessive noun. Then write a sentence using the new phrase. The first one is done for you.*

1. the bright colors of the quilt *the quilt's bright colors*

The quilt's bright colors will make the room look cheerful.

2. the unusual shape of the basket ____________________

____

3. the bird feeder belonging to our class ____________________

____

4. the clubhouse of the members ____________________

____

5. the sweater belonging to the baby ____________________

____

6. the workshop of a blacksmith ____________________

____

7. the rocking horse of the toy makers ____________________

____

8. the needle of the sewing machine ____________________

____

Proofreading Checklist ☑

- ❑ *Did you make singular nouns possessive by adding an apostrophe and -s?*
- ❑ *Did you make plural nouns ending in -s possessive by adding just an apostrophe?*

Unit 2 Review
Lessons 8–11

Common and Proper Nouns (pp. 40–43) *Read each sentence. Write* ***common*** *if the noun in* ***boldface*** *is a common noun. Write* ***proper*** *if it is a proper noun.*

1. The town of **Plymouth** is in Massachusetts. ____________
2. Settlers called **Pilgrims** built the town. ____________
3. **Native Americans** lived nearby. ____________
4. Together, they celebrated a harvest **festival**. ____________
5. The Pilgrims set up long **tables** outdoors. ____________
6. Today, **actors** dress up as the Pilgrims in Plymouth. ____________
7. They act out the first **Thanksgiving**. ____________
8. At the first Thanksgiving, the Pilgrim's showed their **appreciation** for the plentiful harvest. ____________

Singular and Plural Nouns (pp. 44–47) *Read each sentence. Write the plural form of the noun in parentheses.*

9. Most American (family) celebrate Thanksgiving. ____________
10. Traditional (dish) are important in this feast. ____________
11. Stores sell many (turkey) for the main meal. ____________
12. (Box) of pies are piled up on shelves. ____________
13. (Cranberry) are another specialty of the day. ____________
14. Cooks use them to make (sauce) and relishes. ____________
15. Guests arrive from faraway towns and (city). ____________
16. Some (community) have Thanksgiving Day parades. ____________

Irregular Plural Nouns (pp. 48–51) *Read each sentence. Write the plural of the noun in parentheses.*

17. There were ten (child) at our Thanksgiving dinner. ____________________

18. The dining room table was over 16 (foot) long. ____________________

19. All the men and (woman) helped cook the meal. ____________________

20. I couldn't wait to sink my (tooth) into the turkey! ____________________

21. Later, we went outside and saw a flock of (goose). ____________________

22. I asked if a group of (sheep) is also called a flock. ____________________

23. I think a group of (deer) would be a herd. ____________________

24. Ben wanted to know what to call a group of (moose). ____________________

Possessive Nouns (pp. 52–55) *Read each sentence. Write the possessive form of the noun in parentheses.*

25. Have you ever heard (Sarah Hale) name before? ____________________

26. She called attention to (Thanksgiving) importance. ____________________

27. Each (state) date for Thanksgiving was different at one time. ____________________

28. This magazine (editor) idea was to make Thanksgiving a national holiday. ____________________

29. She told some of our (country) leaders of her plan. ____________________

30. Her idea had many (governors) support. ____________________

31. In 1863, Hale even got the (president) attention. ____________________

32. (Abraham Lincoln) proclamation made Thanksgiving a national holiday. ____________________

Unit 2 Test

DIRECTIONS *Fill in the circle next to the sentence that shows correct spelling and the correct use of capital letters and apostrophes.*

1. ○ California is the third largest states.
○ Only Texas and alaska are larger in area.
○ California has the most people.
○ What is this states capital?

2. ○ The Pacific Ocean is just west of california.
○ How beautiful the beachs must be!
○ San Francisco and San Diego are on the coast.
○ These citys have natural harbors.

3. ○ Have you visited the states northern counties?
○ Ranchs, farms, and orchards dot this region.
○ The Napa Valley is known for growing grapes.
○ The redwood trees' grow there.

4. ○ Amazement is your reaction when viewing these many giant tree.
○ Have you heard of Inyo National Forest?
○ The worlds oldest living trees grow there.
○ Tall palm trees line Los Angeles' many boulevards.

5. ○ San Jose is one of Californias' major cities.
○ About 912,000 People live there.
○ Oakland is another Major city.
○ What is Oakland's population?

6. ○ Where is Yosemite national park?
○ The park is 200 miles east of San Francisco.
○ It covers over 1200 square mile's.
○ Some of our Continents highest waterfalls are there.

7. ○ Only small trees and bushs grow in desert areas.
○ Ms. jones's class is learning about desert plants.
○ The class read about Joshua Tree National Park.
○ The childrens want to see this national park.

8. ○ What animals roam California's forests?
○ Deers and foxs all live there.
○ The forests are also the California condors home.
○ Isn't that our countrys' largest land bird?

DIRECTIONS *Read the paragraph, and look carefully at each underlined part. Fill in the circle next to the answer choice that shows correct spelling and the correct use of capital letters and apostrophes. If the underlined part is already correct, fill in the circle for "Correct as is."*

Gold was discovered in California in 1848. News of James Marshall's discovery on the american river (9) spread like wildfire. Thousands of would-be miners from the eastern part of the United states (10) rushed to California. People with "gold fever" also sailed from countrys in europe and asia (11). In all, over 80,000 newcomers arrived in California in 1849. Some found richs, but many miners' lives (12) were filled with hardship. Still, the "forty-niners" liked California and stayed there. Success came to many of those who built businesss, ranchs, and farms (13), turning Sacramento and San Francisco into well-to-do cities (14).

9.
- ○ James Marshall's discovery on the american River
- ○ James Marshall's discovery on the American River
- ○ James Marshall's discovery on the American river
- ○ Correct as is

10.
- ○ eastern part of the united states
- ○ eastern part of the united States
- ○ eastern part of the United States
- ○ Correct as is

11.
- ○ countries in Europe and Asia
- ○ countrys in Europe and asia
- ○ countrys in Europe and Asia
- ○ Correct as is

12.
- ○ found richs, but many miners lives
- ○ found richs, but many miners's lives
- ○ found riches, but many miners' lives
- ○ Correct as is

13.
- ○ businesses, ranchs, and farms
- ○ businesses, ranches, and farms
- ○ businesss, ranches, and farms
- ○ Correct as is

14.
- ○ Sacramento and San Francisco into well-to-do citys
- ○ sacramento and San Francisco into well-to-do cities
- ○ Sacramento and san francisco into well-to-do cities
- ○ Correct as is

Lesson 12: Action Verbs

LEARN

- Every sentence has a subject and a predicate. The **verb** is the main word in the predicate.
- Often, the verb is a word that shows an action. An **action verb** tells what the subject does or did.

Subject	Predicate
The skier	**zooms** down the slope.
Her bright, blue skis	**flashed** in the sunlight.

PRACTICE

A *Read each sentence, and look at the predicate in* ***boldface***. *Write the action verb in the predicate.*

1. The Olympic skiers **gather at the ski slope.** __________
2. They **wear bright, colorful outfits.** __________
3. A fan **cheers for his favorite athlete.** __________
4. Many flags **wave in the breeze.** __________
5. Alpine skiers **race down steep mountain slopes.** __________
6. One skier **moves at a speed of 70 miles per hour.** __________
7. The cross country skier **travels many kilometers.** __________
8. He **glides across the hilly landscape.** __________
9. Ski jumpers **leap long distances through the air.** __________
10. Somehow, they **land on their skis.** __________

B *Draw a line between the subject and the predicate of each sentence. Then write the action verb. The first one is done for you.*

1. Many fans|watch the figure skaters. watch
2. The skaters perform their routines well. ______
3. One athlete traces a figure 8 on the ice. ______
4. She spins in the air. ______
5. The three judges score the events. ______
6. Couples skate as pairs. ______
7. They choose the music for these events. ______
8. Some pairs design their own costumes. ______
9. The male skater lifts his partner high in the air. ______
10. The audience claps loudly. ______
11. Ice dancers move quickly and gracefully. ______
12. The skaters competed in a separate set of events. ______
13. They danced to different kinds of music. ______
14. Judges graded their artistic skills. ______
15. The excited ice dancers waited for their scores. ______

C *Write an action verb to complete each sentence. Choose an action verb from the box, or use an action verb of your own.*

Remember

The **verb** is the main word in the predicate. The verb often shows an action.

change	cheer	covers	enter	lean
look	produces	protect	push	reach
sharpen	signals	sit	swing	wear

1. Speed skaters ________________ tight, lightweight uniforms.
2. They ________________ their skates before each race.
3. Some of these skaters ________________ speeds of 48 kilometers per hour.
4. Helmets ________________ their heads in case of falls.
5. Skating fans ________________ the stadium for the big race.
6. Skaters ________________ forward during the wait for the start.
7. Their eyes ________________ straight ahead.
8. The official ________________ the start of the race.
9. Speed skaters ________________ hard on their skates with each stroke.
10. They ________________ one arm back and forth.
11. A smooth flowing motion ________________ the best skating rhythm.
12. The racers ________________ lanes during a race.
13. Each athlete ________________ the same distance that way.
14. The fans ________________ on the edge of their seats.
15. They ________________ the exhausted winner.

Write Your Own

WRITE

Additional Resources at grammarworkshop.com

D *Read each subject for a sentence. Write a predicate to complete the sentence. Begin each predicate with an action verb. The first one is done for you.*

1. Our town's winter sports festival ___begins today.___

2. Deep snow ______________________

3. The snow sculptures ______________________

4. Some children ______________________

5. A few cross country skiers ______________________

6. A horse-drawn sleigh ______________________

7. Three speed skaters ______________________

8. More snow ______________________

9. Some workers ______________________

10. Two ice dancers ______________________

11. A brave ski jumper ______________________

12. A skater ______________________

13. A fluffy white dog ______________________

14. All the children ______________________

15. Two hockey teams ______________________

Proofreading Checklist ☑

- ❑ *Did you add a predicate to complete each sentence?*
- ❑ *Did you begin each predicate with an action verb?*

Lesson 13: Present-Tense Verbs

LEARN

- The **tense** of a verb tells when an action happens. The action can happen in the present, past, or future.

A verb in the **present tense** tells about an action that happens now or happens often.

Our uncle **drives** a fire truck.
Fire trucks **rush** to a fire.

- A present-tense verb must *agree* with the subject of the sentence. The subject and the verb must both be singular or plural.
  - When the subject is a singular noun or *he, she,* or *it,* add *-s* to the verb.

    A fire **spreads** quickly in a house.
    It **leaps** from room to room.
  - When the subject is a plural noun or *I, we, you,* or *they,* do not add *-s* to the verb.

    Firefighters **save** lives.
    They **protect** property, too.

PRACTICE

A *Choose the verb in parentheses that agrees with the subject. Then write the verb on the line.*

1. A loud siren ________________ in the night. (wail, wails)

2. Two fire trucks ________________ down our block. (roar, roars)

3. I ________________ the flames in a building down the street. (spot, spots)

4. The fire captain ________________ orders to the firefighters. (give, gives)

5. Two women ________________ a hose to the hydrant. (connect, connects)

6. They ________________ the water-filled hose at the fire. (aim, aims)

7. Other firefighters ____________ the front door. (break, breaks)

8. They ____________ the burning building. (enter, enters)

9. The people inside ____________ to the firefighters. (shout, shouts)

10. We ____________ for the best. (hope, hopes)

B *Write the present-tense form of the verb in parentheses to correctly complete each sentence.*

1. A ladder company ____________ next. (arrive)

2. The firefighters ____________ ladders up to the fifth floor. (raise)

3. One firefighter ____________ water into the apartment. (spray)

4. She ____________ yellow flames and dark smoke. (see)

5. A police officer ____________ the street to traffic. (close)

6. She ____________ for backup on her walkie-talkie. (call)

7. I ____________ an ambulance, too. (hear)

8. The ambulance workers ____________ first aid to two people. (give)

9. People ____________ the building with the help of the firefighters. (leave)

10. Families ____________ on the sidewalk. (stand)

11. Fire officials ____________ every part of the building. (check)

12. They ____________ the cause of the fire. (find)

13. The ladder company ____________ all the equipment to the truck. (return)

14. All the emergency workers ____________ the site at last. (leave)

15. We ____________ their brave work! (appreciate)

C *Ms. Wright's class wrote this list of fire-safety tips. The students made nine mistakes in subject-verb agreement. Use the proofreading marks in the box to correct the errors.*

Remember

A present-tense verb must *agree* with the subject of the sentence. The subject and the verb must both be singular or plural.

Proofreading Marks

∧	Add
⊙	Period
ℓ/	Take out
≡	Capital letter
/	Small letter

Smoke detectors save lives!

In your house, each floor need a smoke detector. Test your smoke detectors once a month. The batteries usually lasts about one year.

Fire extinguishers puts out fires!

Small fires grow into big ones. Fire extinguishers stops small fires fast. Keep one in the kitchen and another in the basement.

Fire drills keep families safe!

Many families holds fire drills at their homes. Then each person know the safest way out during a fire. These drills saves lives!

Careful adults hides matches!

Matches are useful, but young children plays with them sometimes. Make sure the matches in your house are in a safe place.

Look Back **Did you correct nine verbs that did not agree with their subjects?**

Revising Sentences

WRITE

D *Verbs show action. If you use descriptive verbs, your readers can see the action more clearly. In each sentence below, change the word in* ***boldface*** *to a more descriptive verb. Write the new sentence on the line. The first one is done for you.*

Additional Resources at grammarworkshop.com

1. I **like** my uncle's work at the firehouse. ______________________

   I (admire) my uncle's work at the firehouse.

2. Some days, he **cleans** the fire truck. ______________________

   ____

3. He **wipes** the equipment, too. ______________________

   ____

4. A loud alarm **sounds** sometimes. ______________________

   ____

5. "Fire!" someone **says**. ______________________

   ____

6. The firefighters **move** toward their trucks. ______________________

   ____

7. To get downstairs, some **go** down a pole. ______________________

   ____

8. Seconds later, the trucks **travel** out the door. ______________________

   ____

9. The fire trucks **head** to the fire. ______________________

   ____

Look Back

Go back to the sentences you wrote. Circle the descriptive verbs you used.

Lesson 14: More Present-Tense Verbs

LEARN

- A verb in the present tense must *agree* with the subject of the sentence. Both the subject and the verb must be either singular or plural.
- Follow these rules to make a present-tense verb agree with the subject.

For verbs that end in *ss, ch, sh, zz,* or *x*:

- Add -*es* when the subject is a singular noun or *he, she,* or *it.*

  press + es = press**es**
  Jackie **presses** a seed into the soil.

  watch + es = watch**es**
  She **watches** the seed grow.

- Do not add -*es* when the subject is a plural noun or *I, we, you,* or *they.*

  The students **press** seeds into the soil.
  They **watch** the seeds grow.

For verbs that end in a consonant and *y*:

- Change *y* to *i,* and add -*es* when the subject is a singular noun or *he, she,* or *it.*

  fly + es = fl**ies**
  A robin **flies** to the oak tree.

  hurry + es = hurr**ies**
  It **hurries** to its nest.

- Do not change *y* to *i* or add -*es* when the subject is a plural noun or *I, we, you,* or *they.*

  Robins **fly** to the oak tree.
  They **hurry** to their nests.

PRACTICE

A *Choose the verb in parentheses that agrees with the subject. Then write the verb on the line.*

1. The students ________________ the signs of spring. (discuss, discusses)
2. My nose ________________ from pollen in the air. (itch, itches)
3. Baby birds ________________ in their nests. (hatch, hatches)
4. Geese ________________ to their spring and summer homes. (fly, flies)

5. We ____________ the birds in the sky. (watch, watches)

6. The air conditioner ____________ on and off. (buzz, buzzes)

7. Pet owners ____________ shedding hair from dogs and cats. (brush, brushes)

8. Mom ____________ the closet for lighter clothes. (search, searches)

9. Fans ____________ to baseball games. (hurry, hurries)

10. The worker ____________ the potholes in the road. (patch, patches)

B *Write the present-tense form of the verb in parentheses to correctly complete each sentence.*

1. Many families ____________ to do spring cleaning in April. (try)

2. Six family members ____________ in old clothes. (dress)

3. Grandma ____________ a broken curtain rod. (fix)

4. George ____________ the windows. (wash)

5. He ____________ them on a stepladder. (reach)

6. The twins ____________ upstairs. (rush)

7. They ____________ the wooden floors. (wax)

8. Ms. Jones ____________ the garage was neater. (wish)

9. She ____________ things in boxes for a garage sale. (toss)

10. Mr. Jones ____________ the curtains in the sun. (dry)

11. Spring cleaning day ____________ quickly. (pass)

12. The adults ____________ at the end of the day. (relax)

C *Jason wrote about baseball tryouts in an e-mail to his aunt. He made seven errors in subject-verb agreement. Use the proofreading marks in the box to correct the errors.*

Remember

A verb in the present tense must *agree* with the subject of the sentence. Both the subject and the verb must be either singular or plural.

I show up for the baseball tryouts every spring, and I tries my best. Baseball is my favorite sport, even though I am not the best player.

When I play left field, I miss a lot of balls. The high ones fly right over me. Fast grounders passes between my legs.

To be honest, I'm not much better at the plate. The ball fly right past me, and I usually strike out. Coach Jim always stress one thing. "Don't tense up at the plate," he says. This time, I relaxes. The pitcher pitch a fastball right toward me. I smack the ball hard, and it sails over the fence.

The other players rushes toward me. I get "high fives" from everyone. Coach Jim tells me the good news. "Congratulations! You made the team," he says. It looks like I am finally on the path to being a great athlete!

Proofreading Marks

^	Add
⊙	Period
ℓ	Take out
≡	Capital letter
/	Small letter

Look Back Did you correct the seven errors in subject-verb agreement?

Combining Sentences

WRITE

Additional Resources at grammarworkshop.com

The verb is the main word in the predicate of a sentence. Sometimes you can combine two related sentences by joining the verbs. Use the word *and* to join the verbs.

Charlie washes quickly. Charlie dresses quickly.
Charlie washes **and** dresses quickly.

Combining sentences in this way will make your writing smoother and clearer.

D *Combine each pair of sentences by joining the verbs.*

1. People play in the park. People relax in the park. ______

2. Sue smells the cherry blossoms. Sue touches the cherry blossoms. ______

3. Children make kites. Children fly kites. ______

4. Karen grabs a football. Karen tosses a football. ______

5. Mia sees the ball. Mia catches the ball. ______

6. Their friends watch them. Their friends encourage them. ______

7. Mr. Ruiz observes the players. Mr. Ruiz coaches the players. ______

Look Back

Go back to the sentences you wrote. Circle the verbs that you joined.

Lesson 15: Past-Tense Verbs

LEARN

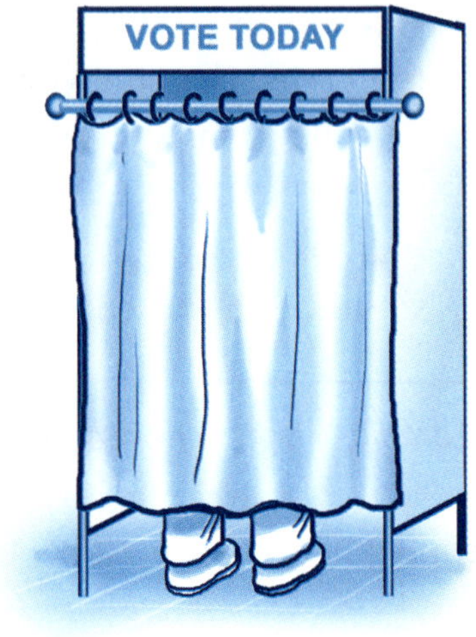

- A verb in the **past tense** tells about an action that already happened.

  The students **elected** a class president.
  I **supported** one of the candidates.

- Follow these rules to form the past tense.
  - Add *-ed* to most verbs.

    help + ed = help**ed**
    All my friends **helped** Will.
  - If a verb ends in *e*, drop the *e* and add *-ed*.

    vote + ed = vot**ed**
    The students **voted** on Tuesday.
  - If a verb ends in a consonant and *y*, change the *y* to *i*, and add *-ed*.

    hurry + ed = hurr**ied**
    They **hurried** to the voting booth.
  - For most verbs that end in one vowel followed by one consonant, double the consonant, and add *-ed*.

    stop + ed = **stopped**
    Our regular schoolwork **stopped** for the election.

PRACTICE

A *Write the past-tense form of each verb.*

1. study ____________________

2. grin ____________________

3. push ____________________

4. debate ____________________

5. reply ____________________

6. answer ____________________

7. decide ____________________

8. play ____________________

9. clap ____________________

10. carry ____________________

B *Write the past-tense form of the verb in parentheses to correctly complete each sentence.*

1. All the students ____________________ in the gym. (gather)
2. Our principal ____________________ the election rules. (explain)
3. I ____________________ Will for class president. (nominate)
4. Will ____________________ his ideas in class meetings. (express)
5. He also ____________________ the other candidate. (debate)
6. Both candidates ____________________ to the front of the room. (step)
7. Will ____________________ TVs in the cafeteria. (want)
8. Chris ____________________ possible school improvement projects. (describe)
9. Most students ____________________ her ideas. (like)
10. The class ____________________ both candidates questions. (ask)
11. I ____________________ a little bit about Will's chances. (worry)
12. Chris's speech ____________________ strong feelings. (stir)
13. We ____________________ a big "get out the vote" drive for Will. (plan)
14. Our teacher ____________________ the votes late Tuesday. (tally)
15. Everyone ____________________ Chris on her victory. (congratulate)

C *Chris wrote this election speech. She spelled eight past-tense verbs incorrectly. Use the proofreading marks in the box to correct the errors.*

Remember

The spelling of some verbs changes when *-ed* is added to form the past tense. Follow the spelling rules when writing the past tense of verbs.

Proofreading Marks

^	Add
⊙	Period
ℓ/	Take out
≡	Capital letter
/	Small letter

My fellow students,

I recently finished a term as your class president, and I tryed to serve you well. I studyed the problems we faced and worked hard to make our school better. I now need another term to finish that work.

Let me briefly describe our class's successes. The first book sale we ever organized raisedd over $200. We used that money for new musical instruments.

The Everyone Can Help program grabed people's attention. More than half of our classmates applyed for volunteer jobs in the school and community.

Our talks with the cafeteria staff helpd, too. Students now have healthier meal choices, and we stoped wasting food.

A few of my campaign ideas appearedd in the newspaper. I hope you read them and will vote for me next week.

Look Back **Did you correct eight spelling mistakes with past-tense verbs?**

Revising Sentences

WRITE

Additional Resources at grammarworkshop.com

D *Read each pair of sentences below. In one sentence, the verb is in the past tense. In the other sentence, the verb is in the present tense. This switch in verb tense can cause confusion for the reader. Write each pair of sentences so that both verbs are in the same tense. The first one is done for you.*

1. The class president **represents** us. She **discussed** important issues with teachers.

The class president represents us. She discusses important issues with teachers.

Or: The class president represented us. She discussed important issues with teachers.

2. The vice president **helped** the president. He **attends** all the class meetings.

3. The class secretary **recorded** notes during meetings. He **reports** news about upcoming events, too.

4. The treasurer **plans** fund-raisers. She **controlled** the class funds.

5. The student government **planned** activities for the class. It **provides** leadership.

Look Back

Go back to each pair of sentences you wrote. Are the verbs in the same tense?

Lesson 16: Future-Tense Verbs

LEARN

- A verb in the **future tense** tells about an action that *will* happen. The action has not yet occurred. Use the special verb *will* to form the future tense.

  The Garcia family **will build** a new house.
  The builder and the Garcias **will discuss** the plans.

- The present, past, and future tenses are called **simple tenses**. They tell about action that happens now, in the past, and in the future.

  PRESENT Ms. Garcia **studies** the plans.
  PAST Ms. Garcia **studied** the plans.
  FUTURE Ms. Garcia **will study** the plans.

PRACTICE

A *Read each sentence. Underline the verb. Circle* **yes** *if the verb is in the future tense. Circle* **no** *if it is not.*

1. The Garcias like the builder's plans.	*yes*	*no*
2. They will call the builder tomorrow.	*yes*	*no*
3. He will supervise the workers at the site.	*yes*	*no*
4. The builder made a schedule already.	*yes*	*no*
5. The schedule shows each part of the project.	*yes*	*no*
6. The whole project will take about three months.	*yes*	*no*
7. Many different workers will order supplies.	*yes*	*no*
8. They haul supplies in their trucks.	*yes*	*no*
9. The family will move in June.	*yes*	*no*
10. They will rent a moving truck.	*yes*	*no*

B *Complete each sentence. Write the future tense of the verb in parentheses*

1. Carpenters ________________ the frame of the house. (build)

2. They ________________ each piece of lumber. (measure)

3. Then they ________________ each wall separately. (construct)

4. These workers ________________ the windows and doorways, too. (shape)

5. The plumbers ________________ next. (arrive)

6. They ________________ the kitchen and bathroom fixtures. (bring)

7. They ________________ the heating system, too. (install)

8. Roofers ________________ on the roof. (work)

9. They ________________ shingles into place. (nail)

10. An electrician ________________ a few weeks at the house. (spend)

11. She ________________ wires through the house. (run)

12. She ________________ the electrical system later. (test)

13. The painters ________________ in early June. (start)

14. They ________________ the inside and the outside of the house. (paint)

15. The Garcias ________________ the colors. (choose)

C *Daniel wrote this entry in his diary. He forgot to put seven verbs in the future tense. Use the proofreading marks in the box to correct the errors.*

Remember

Use the future tense to tell about an action that will happen. Use the special verb *will* to form the future tense.

Dear Diary,

I can't wait until our move next Thursday! We have already packed 30 boxes with dishes, books, clothes, and toys. We probably will pack 30 more before we're done. Mom buy some new furniture for the house after we move in.

Mom and Dad rent a truck next Wednesday. It's a 24-foot truck, so everything will fit. Uncle Jack and Aunt Rita help us load it. They drive the truck over to the new house on Thursday morning. We follow them in our family car.

Once I leave here, I know I will miss my old neighborhood. I miss my friends even more, but I know I come back for a visit. I also know I will make new friends at my new school.

Proofreading Marks

∧	Add
⊙	Period
(take-out mark)	Take out
≡	Capital letter
/	Small letter

Look Back Did you put seven verbs in the future tense?

Write Your Own

WRITE

Additional Resources at grammarworkshop.com

D *This builder's schedule shows the jobs that must be completed by the dates shown. On the lines below, complete the sentences about the jobs on the list. Use* ***will*** *with the verb in parentheses to form the future tense. The first one is done for you.*

May 25	Build cabinets
May 26	Paint rooms
May 27	Install light fixtures
May 28	Pave driveway
May 29	Order kitchen appliances
June 1	Test plumbing system
June 2	Check roof and gutters
June 2–3	Plant bushes
June 3–4	Inspect building
June 3–4	Clean up job site

1. (build) The carpenter *will build the cabinets.*

2. (paint) The painters ______________________

3. (install) The electrician ______________________

4. (pave) A paving company ______________________

5. (order) The builder ______________________

6. (test) The plumber ______________________

7. (check) The roofer ______________________

8. (plant) Landscapers ______________________

9. (inspect) A building inspector ______________________

10. (clean) The work crew ______________________

Proofreading Checklist ☑

❑ *Did you write a future-tense verb in each sentence?*

❑ *Did you use* ***will*** *to form each future-tense verb?*

Lesson 17: Linking Verbs

LEARN

- A **linking verb** links the subject of a sentence with other words that tell about the subject. A linking verb does not show action.

  A shark **is** a meat-eating fish.
  Whale sharks **are** the largest of all sharks.

- Different forms of the verb *be* are often used as linking verbs. Use the form of *be* that agrees with the subject of the sentence.

	Forms of *be*	
Subject	**Present**	**Past**
singular noun *he, she, it*	is	was
plural noun *you, we, they*	are	were
I	am	was

The tank in this room **is** huge.
Those sharks **are** hammerheads.
I **am** curious about sharks.

It **was** open all day.
They **were** popular with visitors.
I **was** busy yesterday.

PRACTICE

A *Read each sentence. Choose the linking verb in parentheses that agrees with the subject. Then write the linking verb on the line.*

1. We ________________ at the aquarium yesterday. (was, were)
2. I ________________ excited about the new shark exhibit. (was, were)
3. The tiger sharks ________________ the biggest. (was, were)
4. One shark ________________ 20 feet long. (was, were)
5. Shark teeth ________________ razor sharp. (is, are)

6. That movie about the great white shark ________________ terrifying! (was, were)

7. Some viewers ________________ afraid of sharks for years. (was, were)

8. Shark attacks on humans ________________ rare. (is, are)

9. The total number ________________ about 100 attacks each year. (is, are)

10. About 20 attacks ________________ deadly last year. (was, were)

B *Write the present-tense or past-tense form of* ***be*** *that correctly completes each sentence.*

1. The giant squid ________________ one of today's rarest sea creatures.

2. Some of its tentacles ________________ 90 feet long!

3. Long ago, sailors ________________ afraid of the giant squid.

4. To them, it ________________ a sea monster.

5. These days, I ________________ very interested in giant squids.

6. Their homes ________________ far below the ocean's surface.

7. Until recently, no photos of these creatures ________________ available.

8. Scientists ________________ unsure of the squid's size for a long time.

9. Some whales ________________ enemies of the giant squid.

10. A deep, round scar on a whale ________________ the mark of a squid attack.

11. The octopus ________________ an ocean dweller, too.

12. It ________________ a shy animal.

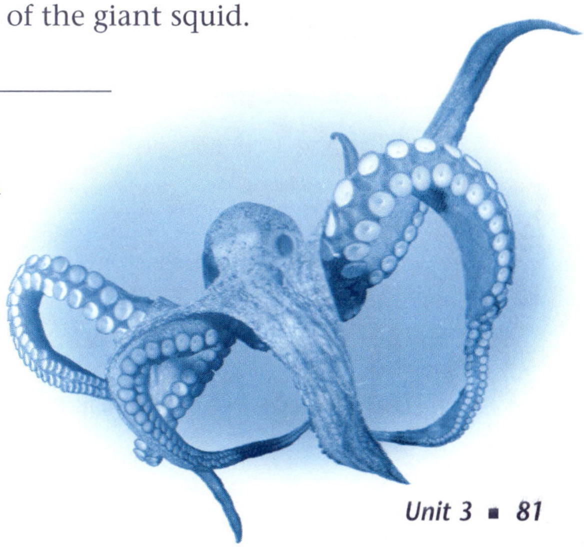

C *Jasmine wrote this report about piranhas. She made eight mistakes using linking verbs. Use the proofreading marks in the box to correct the errors.*

Remember

Different forms of the verb *be* are used as linking verbs. Use the form of *be* that agrees with the subject of the sentence.

Many people is afraid of piranhas. The fear of this fish probably got started because of old movies. In old jungle movies, people was often attacked by hungry piranhas.

In real life, most piranhas is harmless to people. Twenty different types of piranhas live in South America. Many of them eat the fruit and nuts that fall into the water.

Red-bellied piranhas is meat eaters, though. Black piranhas are meat eaters, too. Both of these fish have sharp, pointed teeth, and their jaws is powerful. When the water level is high, these piranhas find plenty of food. They don't bother people.

During dry spells, the water level falls. Then the piranhas is hungrier, and they is more dangerous. Even so, attacks on humans are rare. Of course, we don't have to worry about piranhas in North America. Our climate are too cold for these fish.

Proofreading Marks

^	Add
⊙	Period
⁀	Take out
≡	Capital letter
/	Small letter

Red-bellied piranha

Look Back **Did you correct eight linking verbs?**

Write Your Own

WRITE

Additional Resources at grammarworkshop.com

D *Use a linking verb to join a subject from Box A to a word from Box B, and write a sentence. You can add other words to your sentence, and you can use a choice from a box more than once. An example is done for you.*

A	
the ocean	whales
dolphins	a child

B	
giants	huge
curious	mammals

1. Whales are giants of the sea.
2. ______
3. ______
4. ______

A	
alligators	the animal
jaws	many people

B	
similar	powerful
reptile	afraid

5. ______
6. ______
7. ______
8. ______

Proofreading Checklist ☑

❑ *Did you use a linking verb in each sentence?*

❑ *Did you use the correct form of the linking verb **be**?*

Lesson 18: Main Verbs and Helping Verbs

LEARN

- A verb can be more than one word. In this kind of verb, the most important word is the **main verb**. The **helping verb** usually works with the main verb to tell *when* the action happened. The helping verb always comes before the main verb.

  The moviemakers **are arriving** today.
  They **have unpacked** their equipment.
  They **will shoot** scenes for a movie in our town.

The main verb and the helping verb form a **verb phrase**. In the verb phrases above, the main verbs are *arriving, unpacked,* and *shoot*. The helping verbs are *are, have,* and *will.*

- Here are some common helping verbs.

am	was	has
is	were	have
are	will	had

- The verbs *can, may, must,* and *should* are called **modals**. These verbs are also helping verbs.

  can dance   may sing   must act   should direct

PRACTICE

A *Read each sentence, and look at the verb in* **boldface**. *Write the helping verb and the main verb on the lines.*

	Helping Verb	***Main Verb***
1. The movie company **has hired** a famous director.	________	________
2. The director **is making** an adventure film.	________	________
3. A chase **will occur** in the movie.	________	________
4. Several stunt performers **are preparing** for the scene.	________	________

	Helping Verb	Main Verb
5. The director **may film** the scene today.	________	________
6. The movie stars **should greet** their fans.	________	________
7. People in the crowd **were cheering** for them.	________	________
8. I **am standing** near the cameras.	________	________
9. The director **has planned** every detail.	________	________
10. He **had started** work on the movie months ago.	________	________

B *Underline the verb in each sentence. If the verb is more than one word, be sure to underline both the main verb and helping verb. Then write the verb on the line.*

1. The writers can make some last-minute changes. ________________

2. The director had asked for the changes. ________________

3. The crew tests the equipment. ________________

4. A makeup artist is applying makeup to the stars. ________________

5. Electricians must check the cables before the scene is filmed. ________________

6. Some stunt performers have signaled to the director. ________________

7. An assistant director has requested quiet on the set. ________________

8. The director shouts, "Action!" ________________

9. The cameras are filming the scene. ________________

10. The star jumps into a speedboat. ________________

11. She has practiced this move many times. ________________

12. An exciting chase scene begins. ________________

C *Write a helping verb and main verb to complete each sentence in this e-mail. Choose verbs from the box, or use verbs of your own.*

Remember
A **helping verb** works with the main verb to tell *when* an action happened.

must walk	was explaining	has promised	are filming
have watched	will appear	has scheduled	will begin

Casey,

Something amazing has just happened! As a result, I ______________ (1) in a movie.

As I ______________ (2) to you yesterday, some moviemakers ______________ (3) some scenes here in Fairport. The project is an action-adventure movie. Mom and I ______________ (4) the filmmakers three times this week.

Earlier today, we went down to the marina to watch again. The director saw us and asked if we wanted to be extras in a scene. In the scene, we ______________ (5) down a long dock. When we reach the middle of the dock, a big speedboat chase ______________ (6).

The director ______________ (7) us for 8 o'clock tomorrow morning. Mom ______________ (8) her that we will be there early. Look for me in the near future at your favorite movie theater!

Write Your Own

WRITE

Additional Resources at grammarworkshop.com

D *Write a sentence to answer each question. Include both a helping verb and a main verb in each of your sentences. The first one is done for you.*

1. How many movies have you watched this month? ______

I have watched three movies this month.

2. What movie have you enjoyed recently? ______

______

3. What movie was playing last week in your community? ______

______

4. What actors were starring in the movie? ______

______

5. What movie is showing this week? ______

______

6. Where is the movie playing? ______

______

7. At about what time will this movie start? ______

______

8. Who may join you? ______

______

9. Which actor has created the funniest characters? ______

______

Proofreading Checklist ☑

- ☐ *Did you answer each question with a complete sentence?*
- ☐ *Did you use a helping verb and a main verb in each sentence?*

Lesson 19: Using Helping Verbs

LEARN

- The past tense is often formed by adding *-ed* to a verb. Another way to show a past action is to use the helping verbs *has, have,* or *had* with the past-tense form of the main verb.

  Our grade **has published** a school newspaper.
  The students **have worked** hard on it.
  We **had studied** newspapers in social studies for weeks.

- Be sure to use the helping verb that agrees with the subject of the sentence.

Subject	Present	Past
singular noun *he, she, it*	has	had
plural noun *I, you, we, they*	have	had

PRACTICE

A *Write **yes** or **no** to tell if the helping verb agrees with the subject of the sentence.*

1. Our class has decided to publish a newspaper. __________

2. A few years ago, another class had published a school newspaper. __________

3. We has learned a lot from looking at those earlier news articles and editorials. __________

4. Our staff members have selected Mike and Teresa as the head editors. __________

5. They has asked our teacher for help. __________

6. Each student have volunteered for a job. __________

7. Jon have prepared an article about our new principal, Ms. Gray. ______________

8. He had interviewed her last week. ______________

9. Laura had photographed the new playground. ______________

10. She had borrowed her dad's digital camera for the assignment. ______________

B *Draw a line under the helping verb in parentheses that correctly completes each sentence.*

1. We (has, had) named our paper *The Student News* earlier in the week.

2. Now we (has, have) renamed it *The Dover School Newsflash.*

3. Ginny (has, have) used her layout skills to design the paper.

4. She (have, had) sharpened her skills in a class last year.

5. Finally, I (has, have) finished my article about the cafeteria food.

6. Yesterday, Miki (have, had) asked me to rewrite it.

7. My first draft (have, had) lacked facts and details.

8. Our teacher (has, have) suggested many story ideas to Miki.

9. She (has, have) assigned stories to writers, too.

10. Tim (has, have) roamed around the school looking for news.

11. By last week's deadline, he (have, had) talked to almost everyone.

12. This week, Ramon (has, have) decided to write an advice column.

13. Many classmates (has, have) handed him funny letters to answer.

14. The twins (has, have) edited most of the stories.

15. They (has, have) learned so much about grammar and punctuation.

C *Sasha wrote this news story. In five of the sentences, the helping verbs **has** and **have** do not agree with the subject. Find the mistakes, and use the proofreading marks to correct them.*

Remember
Use *has* with a singular noun and with *he, she,* and *it*. Use *have* with a plural noun and with *I, you, we,* and *they*.

First-Time Racer Wins Pinewood Derby

The Pinewood Derby was held tonight in the school gym. Over two dozen participants entered the race.

Mr. Edward Ryan has held these derby races for 25 years. He have never seen a race with such fast times before.

The big winner is first-time racer Brian Little! He have finished with a best time of 3.15 seconds.

What helped Brian win? Brian says, "I has talked with some winning pinewood racers. They has given me some tips, and tips from good racers help a lot."

By coming in first, Brian have earned the right to go to the regional race in Springfield next month. "I can't wait," he said. In the meantime, he has started to make his car faster!

Proofreading Marks

^	Add
⊙	Period
ℓ	Take out
≡	Capital letter
/	Small letter

Look Back Did you make five helping verbs agree with the subjects?

Write Your Own

WRITE

Additional Resources at grammarworkshop.com

D *Think about something exciting that happened to someone you know. Write seven sentences to tell what happened. Use past-tense verbs with the helping verbs* ***has, have,*** *or* ***had*** *in your sentences. Check a dictionary if you need help spelling a word.*

1. ______________________________

2. ______________________________

3. ______________________________

4. ______________________________

5. ______________________________

6. ______________________________

7. ______________________________

Proofreading Checklist ☑

- ❑ *Did you use* ***has, have,*** *or* ***had*** *with the past tense of verbs?*
- ❑ *Did you use* ***has*** *when the subject of the sentence was a singular noun or* ***he, she,*** *or* ***it****?*
- ❑ *Did you use* ***have*** *when the subject of the sentence was a plural noun or* ***I, you, we,*** *or* ***they****?*

Lesson 20: Progressive Forms of Verbs

LEARN

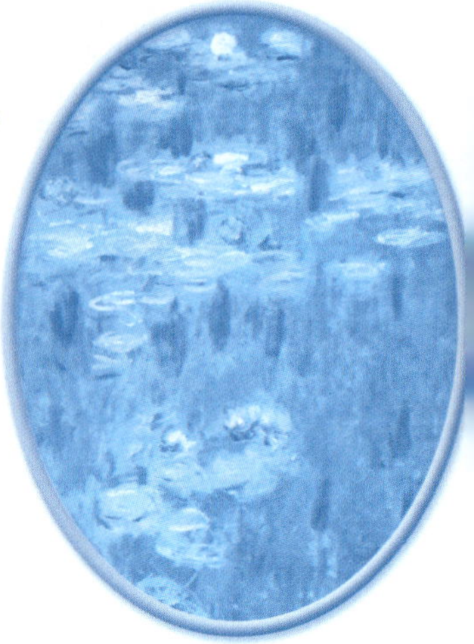

- You have learned about the present, past, and future verb tenses. Each of these tenses has a **progressive form**. The progressive form shows that an action is ongoing.
- The **present progressive** form shows ongoing action that is still happening when the words are written. To form the present progressive, use the helping verb *am, is,* or *are* with the *-ing* form of the main verb.

  I **am studying** about different periods in art.
  Our teacher **is explaining** how an art movement begins.
  Beth and Tom **are looking** at a painting from the Impressionist art period.

- The **past progressive** form shows ongoing action that was happening until another action occurred. To form the past progressive, use the helping verb *was* or *were* with the *-ing* form of the main verb.

  The librarian **was arranging** the books as we entered.
  We **were reading** when the books started to fall.

- The **future progressive** form shows ongoing action that will happen in the future. To form the future progressive, use the helping verb *will be* with the *-ing* form of the main verb.

  Our class **will be discussing** Impressionism this week.

- Notice the subject-verb agreement in the sentences above.

PRACTICE

A *Underline the progressive form of the verb in each sentence.*

1. We are learning about different forms of art.
2. Our art teacher was showing us different ways to hold a paintbrush when the bell rang.
3. We will be painting our own landscapes this week.
4. I am going to the pond near my house to draw.

5. Nick and Luna will be joining me at the pond tomorrow.

6. I was outlining a tree when a duck knocked over my easel.

7. My friends were laughing so hard that no one helped me pick up my painting.

8. Now Luna is sketching a picture of the duck.

9. I am thinking about painting the flowers instead of the trees.

10. Nick will be using the Impressionist style for his landscape.

B *Read each sentence. Choose the helping verb in parentheses that correctly completes the sentence. Then write the helping verb on the line.*

1. Jacob and I __________ working on a presentation on Claude Monet. (is, are)

2. Our librarian __________ gathering art books for us to examine. (is, are)

3. I __________ researching Monet's life and works of art. (am, is)

4. Jacob __________ reading about the start of the Impressionist movement. (is, were)

5. Later, we __________ creating an Impressionist painting of a garden. (was, will be)

6. We __________ preparing a slideshow of Monet's paintings, too. (was, will be)

7. Jacob and I __________ giving our presentation when the fire alarm sounded. (was, were)

8. I __________ walking home when I saw brochure for a Monet exhibit in Paris. (was, were)

9. We __________ talking about Monet's beautiful paintings when Dad came home. (is, were)

10. Now I __________ dreaming about a trip to Paris, the birthplace of Impressionism. (are, will be)

C *Here is a report on the Impressionist painter, Claude Monet. Write the correct present, past, or future progressive form of a verb to complete each sentence. Choose a verb from the box, or use a verb of your own.*

Remember

The **progressive forms** of verbs show ongoing action. To decide which helping verb to add, think about when the action began or will begin.

hope	inspire	learn	live	teach	visit

This month in art class, we ________________ about the Impressionist painter Claude Monet. He is a French painter who lived from 1840 to 1926. While Monet ________________ the Louvre, a museum in Paris, he saw painters copying famous masterworks, like the Mona Lisa. Unlike them, Monet drew what he saw in his own way.

Monet was not the only one in France to paint like this. Others painted this way, too. All these artists ________________ in Paris at that time, and they became friends. Instead of sharp clean lines, the Impressionist painters used rapid, blurred brushstrokes. These artists developed a whole new style of art.

Monet is known for his use of color and the way he painted light. Still today, his artwork ________________ artists to think in new ways. I ________________ to become an artist like Monet. My dream is that one day, I ________________ young artists about his work.

Proofreading Marks

- ^ Add
- ⊙ Period
- ℘ Take out
- ≡ Capital letter
- / Small letter

Write Your Own

WRITE

Additional Resources at grammarworkshop.com

D *Look at the picture below. Using the progressive forms of verbs, write a story based on the picture. Include at least four different progressive forms. Use a dictionary to help with spelling.*

Proofreading Checklist ☑

- ❑ *Did you use **am**, **is**, and **are** for present progressive forms?*
- ❑ *Did you use **was** or **were** for past progressive forms?*
- ❑ *Did you use **will be** for future progressive forms?*

Lesson 21: Irregular Verbs

LEARN

- **Irregular verbs** do not add *-ed* to show the past tense. Instead, the spelling of an irregular verb changes to form the past tense. The spelling of many irregular verbs changes again when they are used with the helping verbs *has, have,* or *had.*

- There are many irregular verbs. Here are ten of them.

PRESENT I **begin** to read Aesop's fables.

PAST I **began** to read Aesop's fables.

PAST WITH *HAVE* I **have begun** to read Aesop's fables.

Present	Past	Past with *has, have,* or *had*
begin	began	has, have, or had begun
bring	brought	has, have, or had brought
come	came	has, have, or had come
do	did	has, have, or had done
eat	ate	has, have, or had eaten
give	gave	has, have, or had given
grow	grew	has, have, or had grown
make	made	has, have, or had made
say	said	has, have, or had said
swim	swam	has, have, or had swum

PRACTICE

A *Write the verb in parentheses that correctly completes each sentence.*

1. A kind butcher had ________________ a hungry dog some meat. (gave, given)

2. The dog ________________ the meat to a bridge over a river. (bring, brought)

3. Before he ________________ to eat, the dog looked down. (began, begun)

4. In the water below the bridge, another dog __________________ into view. (swam, swum)

5. This dog had __________________ to the river with meat, too. (came, come)

6. He stopped and slowly __________________ his meat. (ate, eaten)

7. The dog on the bridge __________________ greedy. (grew, grown)

8. He __________________ a sudden move toward the meat reflected in the water. (make, made)

9. As soon as he had __________________ that, the real meat dropped into the river. (did, done)

10. The hungry dog __________________ nothing that night. (ate, eaten)

B *Write the past form of the verb in parentheses to correctly complete each sentence.*

1. A tired, hungry wolf had just __________________ across a river. (swim)

2. A farmer's dog __________________ barking at the wolf. (begin)

3. "I have __________________ a long way," growled the wolf. (come)

4. "I have __________________ nothing for days," he said. (eat)

5. The kind dog __________________ the wolf some food. (bring)

6. "You must like it here," the wolf __________________. (say)

7. "The farmer has __________________ a lot for me," replied the dog. (do)

8. "What has __________________ that mark on your neck?" the wolf asked next. (make)

9. "I have __________________ so fat that my chain is too tight," explained the dog. (grow)

10. "I would never have __________________ up my freedom for a chain," the wolf said. (give)

C *Evan wrote this version of an old fable called "The Fox and the Goat." He made seven mistakes with the past forms of irregular verbs. Use the proofreading marks in the box to correct the errors.*

Remember

The spelling of an irregular verb changes in the past tense or when used with *has, have,* or *had*.

Fox had fallen into a well. He swum around for a while, but he couldn't get out.

After a while, Goat came along. He had brung a bucket to get some water. "What are you doing down there, Fox?" Goat asked.

Fox looked serious. "Haven't you heard about the drought?" he asked.

Goat gived a shrug. "What drought?" he asked.

"The water shortage has growed really bad all over the country," Fox said. "In fact, this may be the last water left anywhere. If I were you, Goat, I'd jump in!"

Well, the foolish goat done just that. As soon as Goat was in the well, Fox jumped on his back. Then he climbed up onto Goat's horns and out of the well.

"I'm so glad you come along," Fox called down to Goat. "You have maked my day! But next time, look before you leap!"

Proofreading Marks

^	Add
⊙	Period
℘	Take out
≡	Capital letter
/	Small letter

Look Back Did you correct seven mistakes with irregular verbs?

Write Your Own

WRITE

Additional Resources at grammarworkshop.com

D *Complete the sentences in the fable below with past forms of irregular verbs. Use forms of the verbs in the chart on page 96. Then write a few sentences of your own to finish the fable. Use past forms of irregular verbs in some of your sentences.*

The ants were hard workers. All summer long, they had __________ grain and vegetables in their large garden. Once fall came, they __________ the food inside and stored it. They had __________ everything possible to prepare for the cold months of winter.

Grasshopper, on the other hand, __________ very little all summer and fall. When the weather was hot, he __________ in the pond. When he was hungry, he __________ fresh berries off the bushes.

Winter __________ early that year, and Grasshopper __________ to worry. No berries __________ on the bushes now, and he had no food in his house. With his stomach growling, Grasshopper paid a visit to the ants.

"What has __________ you here today, Grasshopper?" asked one of the ants.

____

____

____

Proofreading Checklist ✓

❑ *Did you use the correct past forms of the irregular verbs?*

Lesson 22: More Irregular Verbs

LEARN

- **Irregular verbs** do not form the past tense by adding *-ed*. Instead, the spelling of an irregular verb changes when the past tense is formed. The spelling may change again when the irregular verb is used with the helping verbs *has, have,* or *had*.

PRESENT People **write** tall tales today.

PAST People **wrote** tall tales in the past.

PAST WITH *HAVE* People **have written** tall tales for a long time.

Present	Past	Past with *has, have,* or *had*
break	broke	has, have, or had broken
draw	drew	has, have, or had drawn
drive	drove	has, have, or had driven
fly	flew	has, have, or had flown
ride	rode	has, have, or had ridden
sing	sang	has, have, or had sung
take	took	has, have, or had taken
tell	told	has, have, or had told
throw	threw	has, have, or had thrown
write	wrote	has, have, or had written

PRACTICE

A *Write the verb in parentheses that correctly completes each sentence.*

1. Cowboys have ____________________ tall tales about Pecos Bill. (tell, told)

2. They have ____________________ about how he was raised. (sang, sung)

3. The coyotes ____________________ Bill to the Texas plains. (took, taken)

4. Bill ________________ faster than any other cowboy. (rode, ridden)

5. He ________________ the biggest cattle to market. (drove, driven)

6. No cowboy had ever ________________ a lasso so well! (threw, thrown)

7. One tale has ________________ of a terrible drought. (tell, told)

8. Pecos Bill had ________________ up into the sky on his horse. (rode, ridden)

9. He had ________________ some storm clouds over to Texas. (drove, driven)

10. He ________________ them open so the rain would fall. (broke, broken)

B *Write the past form of the verb in parentheses to correctly complete each sentence.*

1. Almost everyone ________________ railroads in the early 1900s. (ride)

2. People ________________ songs and tall tales about John Henry. (write)

3. Many tales have ________________ about his incredible strength. (tell)

4. Henry ________________ spikes into the wooden boards that hold down railroad tracks. (drive)

5. His huge sledgehammer ________________ through the air. (fly)

6. Some people have ________________ that Henry could swing two hammers at once! (write)

7. A folksinger ________________ about Henry's contest with a new power drill. (sing)

8. Henry's boss had ________________ the drill to the work site. (take)

9. The amazing contest ________________ a large crowd. (draw)

10. Even after the power drill had ________________, John Henry was still working. (break)

C *Sam wrote this story about Paul Bunyan, another hero of many tall tales. Sam made eight mistakes with the past forms of irregular verbs. Use the proofreading marks in the box to correct the errors.*

Remember

The spelling of an irregular verb changes in the past tense or when used with *has, have,* or *had*.

Paul Bunyan throwed down his ax. Then he taked a deep breath. "What a job!" he said. It had took a week, but the giant logger and his big blue ox Babe were finally done. They had cleared the trees out of the Great Forests. People would now call this area the Great Plains.

"To float these logs down to my sawmill in Louisiana," Paul said, "we need a river." Paul hitched a plow to Babe and drived her and the plow down to New Orleans. Believe it or not, that's how the Mississippi River got started!

"Step more lightly," Paul telled Babe. Every so often, her heavy hoofs breaked through the rocky ground, and streams of oil flyed up. Those were the first oil wells.

How do I know these things? Babe told me about them herself, and I have wrote down everything she said.

Proofreading Marks

^	Add
⊙	Period
ℓ	Take out
≡	Capital letter
/	Small letter

Look Back Did you correct eight mistakes with irregular verbs?

Write Your Own

WRITE

Additional Resources at grammarworkshop.com

D *The tall tale below tells what Paul Bunyan might do in today's world. Complete the sentences in the story with past forms of irregular verbs. Use forms of the verbs in the chart on page 100. Then write a few sentences of your own to complete the story. Use past forms of irregular verbs in your sentences.*

Paul Bunyan and the Trees

Last year, Paul Bunyan ________________ across the country in a supersized truck. He ________________ over other areas of the world in a jumbo jet. Along the way, Paul ________________ a long, hard look at the places he passed. What he saw almost ________________ his heart!

Actually, it was the lack of trees that almost ________________ Paul crazy. "People have always ________________ tall tales about my logging," he moaned. "They have even ________________ songs about me and Babe working together. Maybe we have ________________ this logging business too seriously. Now it's time to plant some trees!"

____

____

____

____

Proofreading Checklist ✓

- ❑ *Did you use the correct past forms of irregular verbs?*
- ❑ *Did you use the correct form of the verb with **has, have,** and **had**?*

Lesson 23: Contractions with *Not*

LEARN

A **contraction** is made by joining two words together. An apostrophe (') takes the place of any letters that are left out. Some contractions are formed by joining a verb with the word *not*.

are + not = **aren't**
Some common beliefs about health **aren't** true.

will + not = **won't**
Carrots **won't** improve your eyesight.

Notice that the spelling of the verb *will* changes when it is combined with *not* to form the contraction *won't*

Contractions with *not*			
is not	**isn't**	do not	**don't**
are not	**aren't**	does not	**doesn't**
was not	**wasn't**	did not	**didn't**
were not	**weren't**	cannot	**can't**
has not	**hasn't**	could not	**couldn't**
have not	**haven't**	should not	**shouldn't**
had not	**hadn't**	would not	**wouldn't**
will not	**won't**		

PRACTICE

A *Write the contraction for each pair of words.*

1. was not ____________________

2. cannot ____________________

3. does not ____________________

4. is not ____________________

5. are not ____________________

6. were not ____________________

7. did not ____________

8. had not ____________

9. could not ____________

10. will not ____________

B *Write a contraction for the word or words in parentheses to complete each sentence.*

1. Eating lots of carrots ____________ turn your skin orange. (will not)
2. Worrying ____________ turn a person's hair gray. (does not)
3. Too much chocolate ____________ the cause of pimples. (is not)
4. Foods ____________ cause all skin problems. (do not)
5. Colds ____________ caused by bad weather. (are not)
6. You ____________ get the flu unless you are exposed to a virus. (cannot)
7. Staying in bed ____________ help you get over a cold faster. (will not)
8. Standing on your head ____________ ever cured the hiccups. (has not)
9. Touching a frog ____________ cause warts. (does not)
10. Scientists ____________ found any evidence for this idea. (have not)
11. Everyone wishes you ____________ crack your knuckles. (would not)
12. We ____________ believe every health and diet tip we hear! (should not)

C *Dana and Ian wrote this fact sheet listing other untrue ideas about diet and health. In it, they made eight mistakes with contractions. Use the proofreading marks in the box to correct the errors.*

Remember
When you join two words in a contraction, an apostrophe takes the place of any letters that are left out.

The Truth About Diet and Health

- Drinking coffee won't stunt your growth. Even so, caffeine shouldnt be part of a young person's diet.
- Eating carrots doesnt' improve your eyesight. However, the vitamin A in carrots does help eyes stay healthy.
- Going outside with wet hair wont make you catch a cold. Colds are'nt caused by wet hair or windy weather. They are caused by viruses.
- Watching TV doesnt damage your eyes. However, people who spend too much time watching TV probably dont get enough exercise.
- Reading in dim light isnt a cause of bad eyesight. Good lighting, however, makes reading much easier!
- Crossing your eyes cant' make you permanently cross-eyed. But why do it? It's hard to see that way!

Proofreading Marks

^	Add
⊙	Period
℘	Take out
≡	Capital letter
/	Small letter

Look Back Did you correct eight mistakes with contractions?

Revising Sentences

WRITE

Additional Resources at grammarworkshop.com

D *Read each sentence. Then rewrite it, using one or more contractions formed with **not**. Make any other changes that are necessary for the new sentence to make sense. The first two are done for you.*

1. If you do exercise regularly, you will get in shape. ____________

   If you don't exercise regularly, you won't get in shape.

2. Your scrape has healed because you have taken care of it. ____________

   Your scrape hasn't healed because you haven't taken care of it.

3. My muscles have gotten stronger because I have exercised. ____________

   ____

4. If you do get eight hours of sleep, you will feel rested tomorrow. ____________

   ____

5. If you have eaten breakfast, you will have the energy you need. ____________

   ____

6. Sue did get enough vitamins because she did eat fresh fruit and vegetables. ____________

   ____

7. If you had acted recklessly, you would have gotten hurt. ____________

   ____

8. If you get caught in the rain, you will need an umbrella. ____________

   ____

Proofreading Checklist ✓

- ❑ *Did you use one or more contractions with **not** in each sentence you wrote?*
- ❑ *Did you use an apostrophe in place of letters that are left out?*

Unit 3 Review
Lessons 12–23

Action Verbs (pp. 60–63) *Underline the action verb in each sentence.*

1. Musicians play many different instruments in orchestras.

2. A conductor leads the orchestra.

3. Orchestras entertain people.

Present-Tense Verbs (pp. 64–71) *Write the present tense of the verb in parentheses to correctly complete each sentence.*

4. Ellen (tighten) the strings of her violin. ____________________

5. The clarinet player (remove) his instrument from its case. ____________________

6. The conductor (discuss) the music with the orchestra. ____________________

7. Each musician (study) the music carefully. ____________________

8. The ushers (guide) people to their seats. ____________________

9. My sister (reach) her seat just in time. ____________________

Past-Tense Verbs (pp. 72–75) *Write the past tense of the verb in parentheses to correctly complete each sentence.*

10. Early orchestras (accompany) singers. ____________________

11. Composers (plan) music for more and more instruments. ____________________

12. Some early orchestras (include) more than 100 musicians. ____________________

Future-Tense Verbs (pp. 76–79) *Write the future tense of the verb in parentheses to correctly complete each sentence.*

13. We (go) to a concert next Friday night. ____________________

14. The musicians (play) works by Mozart. ____________________

15. A large crowd (attend) this performance. ____________________

Linking Verbs (pp. 80–83) *Underline the linking verb that agrees with the subject of the sentence.*

16. Drums (is, are) percussion instruments.

17. Another percussion instrument (is, are) the xylophone.

18. I (am, is) a trombone player.

Main Verbs and Helping Verbs (pp. 84–91) *Underline the helping verb in each sentence.*

19. Jamie should distribute the sheet music.

20. The musicians are turning the pages.

21. The conductor will answer our questions.

Progressive Forms of Verbs (pp. 92–95) *Underline the progressive form of the verb in each sentence. Then write it on the line.*

22. Members of the orchestra are playing their scales. ____________________

23. Reilly and Marvin were talking about classical music. ____________________

24. The store will be delivering new music stands. ____________________

Irregular Verbs (pp. 96–103) *Underline the correct verb in parentheses to complete each sentence.*

25. Our orchestra (began, begun) today's practice at two o'clock.

26. All the members have (took, taken) their seats.

27. Jesse had (wrote, written) one of the songs we will perform.

Contractions with *Not* (pp. 104–107) *Read each sentence. Write the words in **boldface** as a contraction.*

28. Some of the instruments **are not** in tune. ____________________

29. We **do not** get discouraged. ____________________

30. Our performance **will not** be perfect until we practice more. ____________________

Unit 3 Test

DIRECTIONS *Fill in the circle next to the sentence that spells and uses verbs or contractions correctly.*

1. ○ Rain clouds has formed in the sky.
○ The wind began to blow harder.
○ Suddenly, the rain splashs down on the sidewalk.
○ A boy hurrys home.

2. ○ The storm has driven everyone indoors.
○ Heavy rain drumed down on our roof.
○ Mom and I didnt close our windows in time.
○ The raindrops varyed in size.

3. ○ The rain has stoped now.
○ The sky have cleared suddenly.
○ A rainbow appear in the sky.
○ Our neighbors may come outside to see it.

4. ○ The rain has provideed the trees and plants with water.
○ It washes the sidewalks, too.
○ Some rain rushs off into streams and rivers.
○ The sun's heat evaporate the rest of it.

5. ○ The clouds have growed dark again.
○ The heavy rain poures down once more.
○ The neighbors has scurried indoors again.
○ We don't like these heavy rainstorms.

6. ○ Snow were falling all night.
○ Snowflakes begun to fall.
○ The snowstorm isnt over yet.
○ The children are throwing snowballs in the air.

7. ○ The roads was icy yesterday.
○ People was driving carefully.
○ My grandmother watch the weather report.
○ We must play indoors today.

8. ○ Our class will made a rain gauge.
○ A rain gauge is a weather tool.
○ It measure the amount of rainfall.
○ Kit has bring a coffee can for the project.

DIRECTIONS *Read the paragraph, and look carefully at each underlined part. Fill in the circle next to the answer choice that shows the correct spelling and use of verbs or contractions. If the underlined part is already correct, fill in the circle for "Correct as is."*

The water cycle supplies (9) Earth with its water. In the cycle, moist air rises from the ground. The moisture takes the form of water vapor, and the vapor is carried high into the sky. Here the air was cooler (10). The cool air cann't hold (11) as much water as the warmer air below. The water vapor changes (12) from vapor into droplets. These tiny droplets forms (13) clouds. Eventually, this moisture will falls (14) to Earth as rain. Snow will fall instead if the temperature has dropped low enough.

9.
- ○ The water cycle supply
- ○ The water cycle supplys
- ○ The water cycle have supplied
- ○ Correct as is

10.
- ○ the air is cooler
- ○ the air are cooler
- ○ the air were cooler
- ○ Correct as is

11.
- ○ cool air cant hold
- ○ cool air can't hold
- ○ cool air can'nt hold
- ○ Correct as is

12.
- ○ The water vapor change
- ○ The water vapor changees
- ○ The water vapor changies
- ○ Correct as is

13.
- ○ These tiny droplets form
- ○ These tiny droplets has formed
- ○ These tiny droplets formes
- ○ Correct as is

14.
- ○ this moisture fall
- ○ this moisture had fall
- ○ this moisture will fall
- ○ Correct as is

Lesson 24: Adjectives

LEARN

- An **adjective** is a word that describes a noun. It can tell *what kind*, and it can also tell *how many*. An adjective usually comes before the noun it describes.

  WHAT KIND We visited a **large** refuge.

  HOW MANY **Several** birds live in the refuge.

- When two or more adjectives describe the same noun, the order in which they appear follows a pattern. Adjectives that describe number come before adjectives that describe size, shape, color, or other qualities.

  Two white swans have built a nest there.

  They used **many dry** twigs to make the nest.

- An adjective can also come after the noun it describes. This usually happens when the adjective follows a form of the verb *be.*

  The swan's nest is **round**.

  The eggs are **white**.

PRACTICE

A *Circle the adjective(s) that describe the noun in **boldface**. Then write the adjective(s) on the line.*

1. A patient **swan** sits on the nest. ____________
2. She protects three small **eggs**. ____________
3. The nest is near a beautiful **lake**. ____________
4. The swan chose a safe **location** for the nest. ____________
5. Tall **grass** surrounds the nest. ____________
6. Few **enemies** bother the birds here. ____________

7. The **eggs** are large. ______________________

8. The babies have sharp **beaks**. ______________________

9. Their beaks break the hard **eggshells**. ______________________

10. Soon the **babies** are free. ______________________

B *Circle the adjective(s) in each sentence, and underline the noun that they describe. Then write the adjective(s) on the line.*

1. Several ducks live near the lake. ______________________

2. Their feathers are waterproof. ______________________

3. Their feet are webbed. ______________________

4. Many hungry ducks dive for food. ______________________

5. They eat insects and small plants. ______________________

6. Their grassy nests are on the shore. ______________________

7. The geese near the lake are noisy. ______________________

8. Their honking is loud! ______________________

9. Five babies may follow an adult. ______________________

10. Their feathers are fluffy. ______________________

11. Nine geese are flying in a pattern. ______________________

12. The pattern is v-shaped. ______________________

13. The geese are watchful. ______________________

14. A goose is fierce at times. ______________________

15. Even the babies are bold! ______________________

Remember
An **adjective** describes a noun.
It can tell *what kind* or *how many*.

C *Write an adjective to complete each sentence. Choose an adjective from the box, or use an adjective of your own.*

beautiful	brown	clear	cute	flat
gentle	green	happy	long	peaceful
sandy	short	soft	sunny	tall

1. We went to the bird refuge on a ____________________ day.

2. The sky above was ____________________ .

3. A ____________________ breeze rippled the water.

4. A ____________________ heron waded along the shore.

5. Its legs were ____________________ .

6. ____________________ water lilies were blooming on the lake.

7. A ____________________ frog sat on a lily pad.

8. Its ____________________ croak faded into silence.

9. Seven ____________________ ducklings were swimming with their mother.

10. We walked down a ____________________ path along the pond.

11. A snake slept on a ____________________ rock.

12. Three ____________________ hawks circled overhead.

13. The ____________________ buzzing of insects filled the air.

14. The bird refuge is so ____________________ .

15. I was ____________________ to be there.

Combining Sentences

WRITE

Additional Resources at grammarworkshop.com

Sometimes you can combine two related sentences into one sentence by moving an adjective.

In the example below, only the second sentence has an adjective. To make one smooth sentence, you can place the adjective *noisy* before the noun *blue jay* in the first sentence.

A blue jay squawked at a squirrel. The blue jay was noisy.
A noisy blue jay squawked at a squirrel.

In this example, both sentences have adjectives. You can combine the sentences by placing the adjective *big* in the second sentence after the adjective *seven* in the first sentence.

Seven turkeys hurried by. The turkeys were big.
Seven big turkeys hurried by.

D *The sentences in each pair below are related. Move the adjective from one sentence to the other to combine the sentences. Write the new sentence on the line.*

1. Two doves rested on a branch. The doves were gray. ______________________

2. A hawk's shadow passed over the lake. It was a dark shadow. ______________________

3. A raven's call broke the silence. It was a harsh call. ______________________

4. The sound echoed across the lake. The sound was mysterious. ______________________

5. We saw different kinds of birds. We saw eight different kinds. ______________________

Look Back

Go back to the sentences you wrote. Circle the adjective or adjectives.

Lesson 25: *A, An, The*

LEARN

- The special adjectives *a, an,* and *the* are called **articles**. These small words come before nouns.

  a raccoon **an** otter **the** animals

- The articles *a* and *an* refer to any person, place, or thing. The article *the* refers to a specific person, place, or thing.

  An elephant can run faster than **a** person.
  The runner crossed **the** finish line at noon.

  - Use *a* before a singular noun that begins with a consonant sound.

    I found **a** book of interesting facts.

  - Use *an* before a singular noun that begins with a vowel sound.

    Each fact described **an** animal.

  - Use *the* before both singular and plural nouns.

    The facts about **the** insect surprised me.

PRACTICE

A *Some sentences have more than one article. Circle each article, and write it on the line. The first one is done for you.*

1. It is impossible for (a) pig to look up into (the) sky. a, the
2. A sleeping bear in winter can go 100 days without water. ________
3. An ostrich never buries its head in the sand. ________
4. There are more than 20 muscles in the ear of a cat. ________
5. An insect buzzes because of the movement of its wings. ________
6. A cockroach can run one meter per second. ________
7. The pattern of a zebra's black-and-white stripes is formed by its hair. ________

8. A snail can sleep for three years. ____________

9. Wolves don't howl more often when the moon is full. ____________

10. A shark's mouth has six to twenty rows of teeth. ____________

B *Write the article in parentheses that correctly completes each sentence.*

1. ________ elephant flaps its ears to stay cool. (A, An)

2. The Chow-Chow is ________ dog with blue lips. (a, the)

3. Some spiders can spin ________ web in 30 minutes. (a, an)

4. A koala is not ________ bear. (a, the)

5. It is ________ relative of the kangaroo. (a, an)

6. Females carry their young in ________ pouch. (a, an)

7. A zorilla is ________ animal that looks like a skunk. (a, an)

Zorilla

8. Zorillas, like skunks, use odor as ________ defense. (a, an)

9. The American buffalo is not ________ buffalo at all. (a, the)

10. It is ________ bison. (a, an)

11. An Andean condor can have ________ wingspan of 10 feet. (a, an)

12. It is one of the largest flying birds in ________ world. (a, the)

13. The world's smallest mammal is ________ bat. (a, an)

14. This tiny bat is the size of ________ bumblebee. (a, an)

15. ________ ostrich is a bird that does not fly. (A, An)

C *Sean wrote a report about how certain animals communicate their emotions. In this part of the report, he used five articles incorrectly. Use the proofreading marks in the box to correct the errors.*

Remember
Use *a* before a singular noun that begins with a consonant sound. Use *an* before a singular noun that begins with a vowel sound.

Does a animal have emotions? That's not easy to answer. How could we tell if animals did feel the emotion? After all, they can't talk. Sometimes, however, animals do express feelings through body language.

For example, if the dog has misbehaved, it might turn its head sideways and show its neck. It might also crouch down and lift its front paw to show you it is sorry. Wolves, which are wild relatives of dogs, might also show these two types of body language.

Wolves live in the pack with one strong leader. Pack members use body language to show that they recognize their leader. To your dog, you are a leader of the pack, so it uses the same kind of body language with you.

Proofreading Marks

^	Add
⊙	Period
℘	Take out
≡	Capital letter
/	Small letter

Look Back Did you correct five mistakes with articles?

Revising Sentences

WRITE

Additional Resources at grammarworkshop.com

D *Write a sentence about each animal below. In each sentence, use an article before the animal's name, and use the information given in parentheses. After writing your sentence, go back and add an adjective to each sentence. The first one is done for you.*

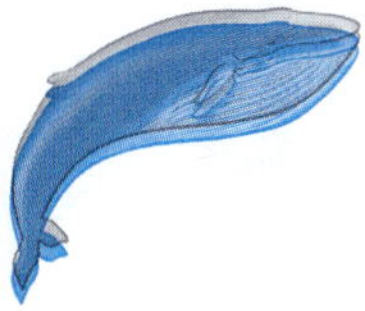

1. blue whale (weighs up to 200 tons)

A blue whale weighs up to 200 tons.

A big blue whale weighs up to 200 tons.

2. butterfly (flaps its wings five times per second)

___

___

3. humpback whale (can eat one ton of food per day)

___

___

4. opossum (sleeps 19 hours per day)

___

___

5. hummingbird (can fly backwards)

___

___

Look Back

Go back to the sentences you wrote.
Circle each article you used.
Underline each adjective you added.

Lesson 26: Demonstrative Adjectives

LEARN

- Adjectives can tell *what kind* or *how many*. Adjectives can also tell *which one*. Adjectives that tell *which one* are called **demonstrative adjectives**.

This, that, these, and *those* are demonstrative adjectives. Use *this* and *that* before singular nouns. Use *these* and *those* before plural nouns.

This film is very popular.
That book is a favorite of young children.
These children are here for Story Time.
Those adults are waiting for them.

- *This* and *these* refer to people, places, or things that are nearby. Do not use *here* after *this* or *these*.

CORRECT The children's librarian has chosen **this book**.
INCORRECT The children's librarian has chosen **this here book**.

CORRECT **These children** want to hold the book.
INCORRECT **These here children** want to hold the book.

- *That* and *those* refer to people, places, or things that are farther away. Do not use *there* after *that* or *those*.

CORRECT Everyone will sit in **that room**.
INCORRECT Everyone will sit in **that there room**.

CORRECT **Those children** want to hear the story again.
INCORRECT **Those there children** want to hear the story again.

PRACTICE

A *Underline the demonstrative adjective in each sentence. Then write it on the line.*

1. The new library is on this block. ____________________

2. It used to be in that old building. ____________________

3. Let's use those computers to search the online catalog. ____________________

4. These books are novels by Laura Ingalls Wilder. ____________________

5. Ask that librarian if you need help to find a book. ____________________

6. These picture books belong in the children's section. ____________________

7. Those volunteers will sort the books by author. ____________________

8. This room is the Listening Room. ____________________

9. Use these earphones to listen to music. ____________________

10. Let's make a reservation to use this equipment again. ____________________

B *Write the demonstrative adjective in parentheses that correctly completes each sentence.*

1. Look at the picture in ____________________ book about New York City. (this, these)

2. It shows ____________________ building across the street. (this, that)

3. ____________________ famous structure is the 42nd Street Library. (That, Those)

4. The library was built on ____________________ two blocks over there. (this, those)

5. Look at ____________________ marble lions at the library entrance. (that, those)

6. ____________________ big cat next to me is nicknamed Patience. (This, That)

7. ____________________ big cat on the other side is nicknamed Fortitude. (This, That)

8. Let's go up ____________________ stone steps and into the main entrance. (this, these)

9. ____________________ magnificent library has eleven reading rooms. (This, Those)

10. Readers can find some useful books in ____________________ reading areas. (this, these)

11. There are 42 oak tables in ____________________ huge room. (that, these)

12. Up to 16 people can sit at each of ____________________ oak tables. (this, those)

C *Angie wrote this script for a tour of the new town library. She made six mistakes when using demonstrative adjectives. Use the proofreading marks in the box to correct the errors.*

Remember

***This* and *these* refer to people, places, or things that are nearby. *That* and *those* refer to people, places, or things that are farther away.**

Proofreading Marks

^	Add
⊙	Period
(take-out mark)	Take out
≡	Capital letter
/	Small letter

Welcome to our new library! We'll begin our tour in the reference section. These here books all around us are reference books. You'll find dictionaries, encyclopedias, and atlases on the shelves. This woman standing over there is Ms. Charles. She is our reference librarian.

In that corner over there, we see the periodical room. Newspapers and magazines are called periodicals. Everyone can go there to read those there magazines and papers.

The library is a great place to do research. These computers against the far wall are for everyone to use. That sheet of paper in my hand lists the rules for computer use.

Finally, here we are in the media section. For many people, that is their favorite part of the library. Audiobooks, videos, eReaders, and eBooks are available. You can borrow them just like books!

Look Back **Did you correct six mistakes with demonstrative adjectives?**

Write Your Own

WRITE

Additional Resources at grammarworkshop.com

D *Imagine you are giving a tour of your classroom from where you sit. Start by listing two things or areas of the classroom that are near you. Then list two things or areas of the classroom that are farther away. A sample is done for you.*

Near	**Farther Away**
the library corner	______________
______________	______________

Now write a sentence with a demonstrative adjective that tells something about the things or areas of the classroom you have listed. You can use the sample below as a model.

1. This area on the left is the library corner. We have books on many subjects on these shelves.
2. ______________
3. ______________
4. ______________

Proofreading Checklist

- ❑ *Did you use **this** and **these** to refer to things that are nearby?*
- ❑ *Did you use **that** and **those** to refer to things that are farther away?*

Lesson 27: Comparing with Adjectives

LEARN

- Adjectives can compare people, places, and things. Adjectives that compare tell how things are different from each other.

  Lions are **stronger** than leopards.
  Lions are the **strongest** big cat.

  - Add *-er* to most adjectives to compare two people, places, or things.

    strong + er = strong**er**

  - Add *-est* to most adjectives to compare more than two people, places, or things.

    strong + est = strong**est**

- Sometimes the spelling of an adjective changes when *-er* or *-est* is added.

  - If an adjective ends in *e*, drop the *e* and add *-er* or *-est*.

    large + er = larg**er** large + est = larg**est**

  - If an adjective ends in a consonant and *y*, change the *y* to *i* and add *-er* or *-est*.

    hungry + er = hungr**ier** hungry + est = hungr**iest**

  - If an adjective ends in one vowel followed by a consonant, double the consonant and add *-er* or *-est*.

    big + er = big**ger** big + est = big**gest**

PRACTICE

A *In Column A, add **-er** to each adjective. In Column B, add **-est** to each adjective. Remember to make the necessary spelling changes before adding **-er** and **-est**.*

	A		***B***
1. cold	____________	**6.** warm	____________
2. wild	____________	**7.** simple	____________
3. scarce	____________	**8.** late	____________
4. tiny	____________	**9.** shady	____________
5. hot	____________	**10.** thin	____________

B *Write the form of the adjective in parentheses that correctly completes each sentence.*

1. Lions are the ________________ members of the cat family. (large)
2. Lions are ________________ than humans. (strong)
3. They can drag ________________ weights than people can. (heavy)
4. They are ________________ than any other cat. (mighty)
5. Lions are not the ________________ of the big cats. (fast)
6. They are usually ________________ than their prey. (slow)
7. A zebra, for example, is ________________ than a lion. (swift)
8. Vision is the ________________ of a lion's five senses. (sharp)
9. A lion can see in ________________ light than you can. (dim)
10. A lion's night vision is ________________ than its prey's night vision. (keen)
11. Hunting at night is ________________ than hunting during the day. (easy)
12. A female lion is ________________ than a male lion. (small)
13. Females are ________________ hunters than males. (fierce)
14. Of all the cats, lions have the ________________ roar. (loud)
15. Many people think that lions are the ________________ animals of all. (grand)

C *Lena wrote this report about tigers. She made seven mistakes when using and spelling adjectives that compare. Use the proofreading marks in the box to correct the errors.*

Remember

Add *-er* to an adjective to compare two people, places, or things. Add *-est* to compare more than two.

Proofreading Marks

^	Add
⊙	Period
ℓ	Take out
≡	Capital letter
/	Small letter

Tigers are an endangered animal. Three kinds of tigers have become extinct. Six other kinds survive. Of these six groups, the larger are the Siberian tigers.

About 400 Siberian tigers are found in Asia. A biger population lives in eastern Russia. These big cats survive in some of the icyest forests on Earth.

Most Bengal tigers live in India, but a smallest population is found in Nepal. Bengal tigers tend to live in the hotest and wettest regions of India.

Indochinese tigers live mainly in the jungles of Thailand. There may be fewwer than 1500 left.

Sumatran tigers are a fourth type of tiger. About 400 of them live on the island of Sumatra. Of all the types, these have the darker coats.

Finally, there are the Malaysian tiger and the South China tiger, the rarest kind. None may be left in China.

Look Back **Did you correct seven adjectives that compare?**

Write Your Own

WRITE

Additional Resources at grammarworkshop.com

D *Follow the directions below to write groups of three sentences. In your first sentence, use the adjective in parentheses. In your second sentence, use the adjective with **-er**. In your third sentence, use the adjective with **-est**. The first one is done for you.*

1. Use the following information about weight to compare these three big cats. (heavy)

Cheetah 160 pounds **Lion** 400 pounds **Siberian tiger** 700 pounds

A cheetah is heavy.

A lion is heavier than a cheetah.

The Siberian tiger is the heaviest of the three cats.

2. Use the following information about top speeds to compare these three cats. (fast)

Leopard 36 mph **Lion** 50 mph **Cheetah** 70 mph

____

____

____

3. Use the following information about body length (including the tail) to compare these three big cats. (long)

Leopard 6 feet **Cheetah** 7 feet **Lion** 9 feet

____

____

____

Proofreading Checklist ✓

- ❑ *Did you use an adjective with **-er** to compare two of the big cats?*
- ❑ *Did you use an adjective with **-est** to compare the three big cats?*

Lesson 28: Comparing with *More* and *Most*

LEARN

The words *more* and *most* are often needed when comparing adjectives of two or more syllables.

- **Use *more* with adjectives when comparing two people, places, or things.**

  Football is **more popular** than soccer in the United States.

- **Use *most* with adjectives when comparing more than two people, places, or things.**

  Soccer is the **most popular** sport in the world.

- **Do not add *-er* or *-est* to an adjective when you use *more* or *most* to compare.**

  CORRECT Jean is **more patient** than Debbie.
  INCORRECT Jean is **more patienter** than Debbie.

  CORRECT Carlos has the **most awesome** kick.
  INCORRECT Carlos has the **most awesomest** kick.

PRACTICE

A *Change each adjective in Column A to compare two. Change each adjective in Column B to compare more than two. Write the new adjectives on the lines.*

A		B	
1. honest	____________	**6.** generous	____________
2. active	____________	**7.** loyal	____________
3. complex	____________	**8.** difficult	____________
4. responsible	____________	**9.** basic	____________
5. famous	____________	**10.** independent	____________

B *Complete each sentence. Add* ***more*** *or* ***most*** *to the adjective in parentheses. Write the words on the line.*

1. Why is soccer the ____________________ game in the world? (popular)
2. Many fans claim soccer is ____________________ than baseball. (exciting)
3. According to them, it is also ____________________ than football. (enjoyable)
4. Soccer is the ____________________ game I have ever played. (active)
5. In football, breaks in the action are ____________________ than in soccer. (frequent)
6. Nonstop action is soccer's ____________________ feature. (appealing)
7. Other sports have ____________________ rules than soccer. (complicated)
8. The rules for football are probably the ____________________ of all. (complex)
9. As a result, football is ____________________ to learn than soccer. (challenging)
10. Soccer also has the ____________________ equipment of any team sport. (basic)
11. That helps make it the ____________________ sport of all. (affordable)
12. Baseball equipment is ____________________ than soccer equipment. (expensive)
13. Setting up a football field is ____________________ than setting up a soccer field. (demanding)
14. Soccer fans may be the ____________________ sports fans in the world. (spirited)
15. They may also be the ____________________ fans in the world. (loyal)

C *Eric wrote this journal entry about playing soccer. He made six mistakes when he used adjectives to compare. Use the proofreading marks in the box to correct the errors.*

Remember
Do not add *-er* or *-est* to an adjective when you use *more* or *most* to compare.

Everyone wants to win at soccer. Winning, however, is not my most importantest goal. Learning teamwork, playing fairly, and having fun are my main reasons for playing. To me, being in top shape is a more importanter goal than being on the top team.

Of the dozens of soccer leagues in the state, ours has the best teams. We play against the most skillfullest athletes in our age group. Win or lose, I enjoy the competition. And when the season is over, I know I've improved. My passes are most accurate than before, and I understand the game a little better.

Now that the season is about to start, I am looking forward to the more exciting year the team has ever had. Even though I play mainly for the love of the game, I also hope it is the more successful season ever!

Proofreading Marks

^	Add
⊙	Period
(loop)	Take out
≡	Capital letter
/	Small letter

Look Back Did you correct six mistakes in adjectives that compare?

Write Your Own

WRITE

Additional Resources at grammarworkshop.com

D *Write three sentences to compare the three sports in each group. In your first sentence, use the adjective in parentheses. In your second sentence, use **more** with the adjective. In your third sentence, use **most** with the adjective. The first one is done for you.*

1. tennis baseball golf (exciting)

Golf is exciting to watch.

Tennis is more exciting than golf.

Baseball is the most exciting of the three sports.

2. kickball dodgeball softball (enjoyable)

____

____

____

3. basketball hockey football (challenging)

____

____

____

4. diving figure skating swimming (graceful)

____

____

____

Proofreading Checklist ☑

- ❑ *Did you use **more** with an adjective to compare two sports?*
- ❑ *Did you use **most** with an adjective to compare three sports?*

Lesson 29: Comparing with *Good* and *Bad*

LEARN

- The adjectives *good* and *bad* have special forms for comparing.

Adjective	Compare Two	Compare More Than Two
good	better	best
bad	worse	worst

- Use *better* when comparing two people, places, or things. Use *best* when comparing more than two.

    A dog makes a **good** pet.
    A cat makes a **better** pet than a dog.
    A parrot makes the **best** pet of all.

- Use *worse* when comparing two people, places, or things. Use *worst* when comparing more than two.

    The rain brought **bad** weather.
    The sleet brought **worse** weather.
    The ice storm brought the **worst** weather of all.

PRACTICE

A *Underline the form of* ***good*** *or* ***bad*** *in each sentence. Then write the word on the line.*

1. Walking my dog Lucky is the best way for me to exercise. ____________
2. Walking Lucky is better than playing softball. ____________
3. Lucky and I took the worst shortcut to the park. ____________
4. The path was worse than the road we always take. ____________
5. It was the worst idea I ever had. ____________

*Write the form of **good** or **bad** in parentheses that correctly completes each sentence.*

6. Our pet rabbit did the ________________ thing yesterday. (worse, worst)

7. Was it ________________ than what he did last week? (worse, worst)

8. Eating flowers in the garden was the ________________ thing he ever did. (worse, worst)

9. We must put a ________________ fence around the flower bed. (better, best)

10. The ________________ kind of fence is one with no openings. (good, best)

B *Write the form of the adjective in parentheses that correctly completes each sentence.*

1. The forest is the ________________ place to see woodland animals. (good)

2. Morning is a ________________ time of day to see a deer. (good)

3. A hot afternoon is the ________________ time. (bad)

4. Did you know that some flowers have a ________________ smell? (bad)

5. The ________________ ones of all smell like rotting meat. (bad)

6. This ________________ odor attracts flies. (bad)

7. Is the odor ________________ than the odor of a skunk? (bad)

8. Look up to get an even ________________ view of the birds. (good)

9. This trail leads to the ________________ spot for bird-watching. (good)

10. It is a ________________ trail than the rocky one. (good)

11. This picture of the rabbit is ________________ than the first one. (bad)

12. Still, it is ________________ than the picture of the woodpecker. (good)

C *Martin wrote this report about a class trip. He made six mistakes using the different forms of **good** and **bad**. Use the proofreading marks in the box to correct the errors.*

Remember

Use *better* and *worse* to compare two people, places, or things. Use *best* and *worst* to compare more than two people, places, or things.

Last week, our class visited the new aquarium. It has the better exhibit of ocean life I've ever seen.

During our visit, we had the best tour ever. First, our tour guide took us to see a film about rare and dangerous animals. Then she took us to see something even best than the tour. She led us to a circular fish tank that had a spiral ramp wrapped around it. The tank was four floors high and filled with a variety of fish, sharks, and sea turtles. It was awesome! Unfortunately, I was standing next to a baby carriage. The baby inside was crying really loudly. It was the worse spot of all to be standing. Then I saw that Paula's spot was worst than mine. She was standing behind a man who was 6 feet tall!

I really enjoyed this class trip. The better part was watching a diver feed the animals in the tank. The worse part was having to leave the aquarium.

Proofreading Marks

∧	Add
⊙	Period
ℓ	Take out
≡	Capital letter
/	Small letter

Look Back Did you correct six forms of *good* and *bad*?

Write Your Own

WRITE

Additional Resources at grammarworkshop.com

D *Write about a trip you took with your class. Tell where you went and what you saw. Describe the best part and worst part of the trip. Include the words* ***better***, ***best***, ***worse***, *and* ***worst*** *in your descriptions. Check a dictionary if you need help spelling a word.*

Proofreading Checklist ☑

- ❑ *Did you use* ***better*** *and* ***worse*** *to compare two people, places, or things?*
- ❑ *Did you use* ***best*** *and* ***worst*** *to compare more than two?*

Lesson 30: Adverbs

LEARN

- An **adverb** is a word that generally describes a verb. Adverbs describe verbs by telling *how, when,* or *where* an action happens. Many adverbs end in *-ly*.

HOW	The news reporters work **hard**. They check the facts **carefully**.
WHEN	The evening news will begin **soon**. The team **always** prepares in advance.
WHERE	The news van rushes **ahead**.

Notice that adverbs can come before or after the verbs they describe.

- Here are some adverbs that tell *how*.

slowly	suddenly	quietly	well	badly
fast	together	hard	easily	quickly

- Here are some adverbs that tell *when*.

yesterday	often	always	then	usually
next	tomorrow	later	soon	recently

- Here are some adverbs that tell *where*.

here	there	outside	below	near
upstairs	locally	everywhere	ahead	far

PRACTICE

A *Circle the adverb that describes the verb in* **boldface**. *Write whether the adverb tells* **how, when,** *or* **where**.

1. Aunt Sonia always **wanted** to be a reporter. ______________
2. She recently **got** her wish. ______________
3. Today, she **is** a reporter at a TV news studio. ______________
4. Many other reporters **work** there with her. ______________
5. The news director **plans** the assignments carefully. ______________

6. Aunt Sonia often **interviews** people. ____________________

7. She **tries** hard to ask good questions. ____________________

8. She **travels** everywhere for stories. ____________________

9. A camera crew usually **follows** her. ____________________

10. Later, she **writes** the news story. ____________________

B *Circle the adverb in each sentence, and underline the verb that it describes. Then write the adverb on the line.*

1. Aunt Sonia visited city hall recently. ____________________

2. Her news crew went there to cover the city spelling bee. ____________________

3. Over 100 students usually enter the event. ____________________

4. I gladly participated in the spelling bee. ____________________

5. I was always a good speller. ____________________

6. I bravely attempted each spelling. ____________________

7. I spelled many words correctly. ____________________

8. My aunt smiled happily. ____________________

9. One student finally won the bee. ____________________

10. Everyone clapped wildly for the winner. ____________________

11. Aunt Sonia interviewed the winner afterwards. ____________________

12. Then she interviewed some other students. ____________________

13. The camera crew filmed steadily. ____________________

14. I looked directly into the camera. ____________________

15. Watch for me tonight on the news. ____________________

Remember An **adverb** describes a verb by telling *how, when,* or *where* an action happens.

C *Write an adverb to complete each sentence. Choose an adverb from the box, or use an adverb of your own. The clue in parentheses will help you. The first one is done for you.*

clearly	fairly	far	locally	next	usually

1. News reporters must describe events ___clearly___. (how)
2. They must also present stories ________________. (how)
3. Facts are ________________ double-checked at the studio. (when)
4. News editors decide which stories to cover ________________. (when)
5. Reporters might investigate stories ________________ or nationally. (where)
6. They might travel near or ________________ for a story. (where)

always	anywhere	correctly	quickly	sometimes	well

7. News video can take viewers ________________. (where)
8. The video should work ________________ with the story. (how)
9. A news anchorperson ________________ reads the news. (when)
10. A good anchor reads each story ________________. (how)
11. The anchor ________________ interviews people on air. (when)
12. Thanks to the news broadcast, we ________________ learn what is happening. (how)

Revising Sentences

WRITE

D *Adverbs make sentences clearer and more interesting. Read these sentences from a news report about a snowstorm. Then rewrite each one, adding an adverb. Your adverb should tell how, when, or where an action happens. The first one is done for you.*

Additional Resources at grammarworkshop.com

1. The worst snowstorm in 40 years hit Riverview. ______________________

The worst snowstorm in 40 years hit Riverview yesterday.

2. The snow fell for over 24 hours. ______________________

____

3. Snowplows are working to clear the streets. ______________________

____

4. All city schools will close. ______________________

____

5. City officials are checking weather reports. ______________________

____

6. More snow and strong winds will arrive. ______________________

____

7. Also, temperatures are falling. ______________________

____

8. We can't expect any relief! ______________________

____

Look Back

Go back to the sentences you wrote. Circle the adverbs that you added.

Lesson 31: Comparing with Adverbs

LEARN

- An **adverb** can compare two or more actions.
  - Add *-er* to most one-syllable adverbs to compare two actions.
    Jason runs **faster** than I do.
  - Add *-est* to most one-syllable adverbs to compare more than two actions.
    Tran runs **fastest** of all the students in our class.
- The words *more* and *most* can also be used with adverbs to compare. Use *more* and *most* with most adverbs that have two or more syllables, including adverbs that end in *-ly*.
  - Use *more* with adverbs to compare two actions.
    Ian leaps **more gracefully** than Tai.
  - Use *most* with adverbs to compare more than two actions.
    Of all the athletes in our school, Megan leaps **most gracefully**.
  - Do not add *-er* or *-est* to an adverb when you use *more* or *most*.

PRACTICE

A *Write the adverb in parentheses that correctly completes each sentence.*

1. Our track club practices ________________ in spring than in winter. (harder, hardest)

2. Saturday is the day we begin ________________. (earlier, earliest)

3. Today, I jogged ________________ than I did yesterday. (longer, longest)

4. Beginners should run ________________ than experienced runners. (more slowly, most slowly)

5. Of all the members in our club, Sonia can jump ________________. (higher, highest)

PRACTICE **A** *continued*

6. Runners must breathe ________________ than walkers. (more deeply, most deeply)

7. I run ________________ on grass than on the sidewalk. (more comfortably, most comfortably)

8. Of all the club runners, Alex practices ________________. (more frequently, most frequently)

9. Of the three clubs, ours trains ________________ for the 5-kilometer race. (more seriously, most seriously)

10. We have competed ________________ than we did last year. (more successfully, most successfully)

B *Write the form of the adverb in parentheses that correctly completes each sentence.*

1. Of the eight runners in the 100-meter race, Alberto ran

   ________________. (fast)

2. I sprinted ________________ than Neil did. (quickly)

3. The high jump took ________________ to organize than the 5-kilometer race. (long)

4. I've practiced ________________ this year than last year. (hard)

5. Fans cheered ________________ for the long jump than for the 5-kilometer race. (loud)

6. Of all the races, I cheered ________________ for the relay. (wildly)

7. In the long jump, Nilda jumped ________________ than Rachel. (confidently)

8. Of the many sprinters, Lin ran ________________. (rapidly)

9. She certainly ran ________________ than I did. (smoothly)

10. I hope our team performs ________________ than any other team. (impressively)

C

Jenna wrote this story for the sports section of her school newspaper. She made six mistakes when using adverbs that compare. Use the proofreading marks in the box to correct the errors.

Remember

Add *-er* or *-est* to most one-syllable adverbs to compare. Use *more* or *most* with most adverbs that have two or more syllables.

Proofreading Marks

^	Add
⊙	Period
℘	Take out
≡	Capital letter
/	Small letter

The Track and Field Festival at Town Park on April 1 was a big success. Of the three track clubs, the Lions performed more successfully. "All the athletes performed more skillfully than last year," Coach Chen said.

Over twelve runners took part in the 5-kilometer race. Jan Ruiz ran most fastest. As usual, she also ran the most gracefully of all the athletes.

Tom Powers took first prize in the high jump, jumping more higher than he did in his record jump. Of the many athletes in the long jump, Carla Allen jumped farther.

All three clubs had teams in the relay race. The Aces ran fastest. They also handed off the baton more smoothlier than the Trackers.

A large crowd gathered, and people cheered more loudlier as the day went on. All in all, the future of track in this town looks bright!

Look Back **Did you correct six mistakes in adverbs that compare?**

Write Your Own

WRITE

Additional Resources at grammarworkshop.com

D *Write two sentences to describe what is happening in each picture. Use the adverbs in parentheses to compare the actions of the athletes.*

1. (fast) ______________________________

____

2. (gracefully) ______________________________

____

3. (high) ______________________________

____

4. (impressively) ______________________________

____

Proofreading Checklist ✓

- ❑ *Did you add* ***-er*** *or* ***–est*** *to the one-syllable adverbs?*
- ❑ *Did you use* ***more*** *or* ***most*** *with the adverbs that have two or more syllables?*

Lesson 32: Using *Good* and *Well*

LEARN

The words *good* and *well* can sometimes be confusing.

Good is an adjective that describes a noun.

Kim is a **good** cook.

Well is usually an adverb that describes a verb.

She bakes **well**, too.

Well is an adjective only when it refers to someone's health. When *well* refers to health, it describes a noun.

Kim was sick. She is **well** now.

Think about what you are describing when using *good* and *well.*

PRACTICE

A *Underline the word in parentheses that correctly completes each sentence.*

1. I'm afraid I don't cook very (good, well).
2. I thought I could make a (good, well) dinner from frozen leftovers.
3. I had promised my family a (good, well) meal.
4. Unfortunately, I didn't plan (good, well).
5. I should have taken a (good, well) look at the frozen foods.
6. I needed more time to cook them (good, well).
7. My cooking did not make a (good, well) impression on the family.
8. Fortunately, Dad had a (good, well) idea.

9. He knew that the microwave oven in the apartment next door worked (good, well).

10. We managed to cook the food quickly, thanks to our (good, well) neighbors.

B *Write **good** or **well** to complete each sentence.*

1. All young people should learn how to eat ________.
2. Cooking is a ________ skill to have.
3. Home-cooked, healthful meals help you stay ________.
4. Fast food from a restaurant isn't generally a ________ choice.
5. Cooking at home is a ________ way to save money.
6. Nutritious meals help a sick person get ________.
7. Making a ________ meal is relaxing.
8. There are many ________ ways to learn to cook.
9. Everyone knows at least one ________ cook.
10. Spend time with someone who cooks ________.
11. TV chefs prepare food very ________, too.
12. Reading cookbooks is another ________ idea.
13. In time, you will have many ________ recipes.
14. You will learn to serve meals ________.
15. There are plenty of ________ reasons to learn how to cook.

C *Christopher wrote this restaurant recommendation for his aunt. He made six mistakes when using the words* ***good*** *and* ***well****. Use the proofreading marks in the box to correct the errors.*

Remember

Good is an adjective that describes a noun. *Well* is usually an adverb that describes a verb.

Proofreading Marks

- ^ Add
- ⊙ Period
- Take out
- ≡ Capital letter
- / Small letter

If you're looking for a well restaurant, try the Lakeview House.

First of all, the owners did a good job with decorating. Old signs and photographs cover the walls. Most nights, a jazz band plays. The bands play good, and the music goes good with the lakefront location. My mother wasn't feeling that well when we arrived, but the music soon cheered her up.

There's always a good atmosphere at the Lakeview House. The waiters always treat the customers well. Most tables have a well view of the lake, too.

Now for the most important thing—the food. My fish was delicious. It was cooked really good. Even the salad was good. Mom said her grilled chicken was good, too.

The next time you want to eat out, try the Lakeview House. I think you'll have a well opinion of it, too.

Look Back Did you correct six mistakes with *good* and *well*?

Write Your Own

WRITE

D *Imagine you are talking to a friend about food. Write two sentences you would say about each topic below. Use the word in parentheses in each sentence.*

1. your favorite fruit or vegetable

(good) ______________________________

(well) ______________________________

2. your favorite sandwich

(good) ______________________________

(well) ______________________________

3. your favorite home-cooked meal

(good) ______________________________

(well) ______________________________

4. your favorite dessert

(good) ______________________________

(well) ______________________________

Now imagine you are a nutritionist writing an article about healthy eating. How might the sentences you write for the article be different from the sentences above? Discuss this question with your classmates.

Additional Resources at grammarworkshop.com

Proofreading Checklist ☑

- ❑ *Did you use the word **good** to describe nouns?*
- ❑ *Did you use the word **well** to describe verbs or to refer to someone's health?*

Lesson 33: Negatives

LEARN

- A word that means "no" is called a **negative**. The words *no, not, nothing, none, never, nowhere, nobody,* and *no one* are negatives.

  Good manners **never** go out of style.
  There is **no** reason to behave rudely.

- Contractions with *not,* such as *don't, wasn't,* and *aren't,* are also negatives.

  Many people **aren't** polite enough.
  They **don't** think about other people's feelings.

- Do not use two negatives together in a sentence. This kind of mistake is called a **double negative**. To correct a sentence with a double negative, take out one negative or replace it with a word such as *any, every, ever, anything, anywhere, anyone,* or *anybody*.

INCORRECT	**Don't never** talk during a movie.
CORRECT	**Don't** talk during a movie.
	Never talk during a movie.
	Don't ever talk during a movie.

PRACTICE

A *Write the negative word in each sentence.*

1. Don't interrupt a speaker. ____________
2. Try not to call out answers in class. ____________
3. Booing another team doesn't show good sportsmanship. ____________
4. Nobody likes to lose a game. ____________
5. Still, there's nothing worse than a sore loser! ____________
6. There is no excuse for bad behavior. ____________
7. Never forget to say, "Please" and "Thank you." ____________

8. You shouldn't expect others to clean up after you. ____________________

9. None of us should forget to write thank-you notes. ____________________

10. There isn't any substitute for good manners. ____________________

B *Write the word in parentheses that correctly completes each sentence.*

1. When it comes to manners, there isn't ____________________ as important as the dinner table. (anywhere, nowhere)

2. Don't go ____________________ too far when dinnertime is near. (anywhere, nowhere)

3. There isn't ____________________ in the kitchen. (no one, anyone)

4. No one ____________________ start eating before everyone is served. (should, shouldn't)

5. You should not ____________________ eat too fast. (ever, never)

6. There's never ____________________ excuse for gulping down food. (no, any)

7. Don't reach for ____________________ over someone else's plate. (nothing, anything)

8. Sometimes you don't like ____________________ on your plate. (nothing, anything)

9. Still, nobody wants to hear ____________________ rude comments about the food. (no, any)

10. You shouldn't ____________________ chew with your mouth open. (ever, never)

11. There shouldn't be ____________________ elbows on the table. (any, no)

12. There isn't ____________________ who can cook this well. (nobody, anybody)

C *Mariah wrote this essay about why manners are important. She used seven double negatives in her writing. Use the proofreading marks in the box to correct the errors.*

Remember

Do not use two negative words together in a sentence. This kind of mistake is called a double negative.

Proofreading Marks

^	Add
⊙	Period
ℓ/	Take out
≡	Capital letter
/	Small letter

A lot of people today don't have no manners. They think that manners don't matter. That's where they're wrong.

Manners aren't just saying, "Please," or waiting your turn in line. Manners are about being kind and thoughtful. You don't want no one to interrupt you, so you shouldn't interrupt nobody else. It isn't no fun having someone cut in line in front of you, so you should never cut in front of nobody else.

People will judge you by your manners. If you don't have none, people will not think well of you. Even simple actions like saying, "Thank you," will make a good impression on others.

Good manners alone have never made no one a success. On the other hand, they haven't ever hurt anyone.

Look Back Did you correct seven double negatives?

Revising Sentences

WRITE

Additional Resources at grammarworkshop.com

D *Rewrite each sentence by adding a negative. Your sentences should give rules for good manners online. There may be more than one way to change each sentence. The first one is done for you.*

1. It's a good idea to type e-mails in all capital letters. It's not a good idea to type e-mails in all capital letters. Or: Don't type e-mails in all capital letters.

2. People who type in all capital letters are being thoughtful. ______________________

____

3. Use busy-looking, colorful type and backgrounds in your e-mails. ______________________

____

4. Busy-looking e-mails are easy to read. ______________________

____

5. Leave the "Subject" line in an e-mail blank. ______________________

____

6. Some people want to receive e-mail jokes and chain letters. ______________________

____

7. Most of us want our mailboxes filled with junk mail. ______________________

____

8. Open e-mails from people you don't know. ______________________

____

Proofreading Checklist ☑

- ❑ *Did you add a negative to each sentence you wrote?*
- ❑ *Did you avoid double negatives in your sentences?*

Lesson 34: Prepositions and Prepositional Phrases

Snowshoe hare

LEARN

- A **preposition** is a word that shows how a noun or pronoun is connected to some other word in the sentence.

  The snowshoe hare lives **in** Alaska.
  During the summer, the hare's coat is brown.
  The hare's brown coat blends **with** the ground.

Here are some common prepositions.

about	among	below	for	near	through
above	around	beside	from	of	to
across	at	by	in	off	under
after	before	down	inside	on	until
against	behind	during	into	over	with

- A **prepositional phrase** is a group of words that begins with a preposition and ends with a noun or pronoun. When a prepositional phrase comes at the beginning of a sentence, it is followed by a comma.

  After the first snowfall, the hare's coat turns white.
  The hare **with the white coat** eats its meal.
  Another snowshoe hare sits **beside it**.

Prepositional phrases add important and interesting information to sentences.

PRACTICE

A *Read each sentence. Look at each prepositional phrase in* ***boldface****. Write the preposition on the line.*

1. I read a book **about camouflage**. ____________

2. Camouflage lets an animal hide **from its predators**. ____________

3. The chameleon lives **in Asia and Africa**. ____________

4. **Among green leaves**, this lizard turns green. ____________

5. **Above a brown branch**, it turns brown. ____________

6. A giraffe has dark blotches **on its coat**. ____________

7. These blotches look like patches **of shade**. ____________

8. The giraffe is hard to see **under trees**. ____________

9. A fawn **with spots** is also hard to see. ____________

10. Light and shadows hide it **from view**. ____________

B *Underline the prepositional phrase in each sentence. Then write the preposition on the line.*

1. Some predators catch prey by surprise. ____________

2. Camouflage helps many of them. ____________

3. Frogs are hard to see on a green riverbank. ____________

4. They wait there for insects. ____________

5. The leaf-tailed gecko moves across the forest floor. ____________

6. To an insect, it could be a leaf. ____________

7. The arctic fox is white during the winter months. ____________

8. Quietly, it creeps over the snow. ____________

9. Fish below the water's surface can see the white feathers that cover a penguin's belly. ____________

10. These feathers look like the top of the water. ____________

11. This area gets bright light from the sun. ____________

12. Under the water, fish don't notice the penguin. ____________

C *Write a prepositional phrase to complete each sentence. Choose a prepositional phrase from the box, or use a prepositional phrase of your own. The first one is done for you.*

Remember
A **prepositional phrase** is a group of words that begins with a preposition and ends with a noun or pronoun.

in the dry grass	on the African plains	in snowy places
down a river	against the snow	for a drink

1. Lion cubs live on the African plains.
2. Their sandy-colored coats help them hide ______
3. Harp seal cubs live ______
4. Their snow-white coats can't be seen ______
5. A crocodile looks like a log floating ______
6. The crocodile doesn't move until some prey stops ______

against the sand	in a swamp	with long necks
in muddy water	of the desert	on its back

7. The turtle carries its home ______
8. ______, this shell looks like a rock.
9. Many desert birds are the color ______
10. Their enemies can't see them ______
11. Many swamp birds have thin bodies ______
12. These birds look like reeds ______

Revising Sentences

WRITE

Additional Resources at grammarworkshop.com

D *One way to make a sentence more interesting and helpful to a reader is to add a prepositional phrase. Add a prepositional phrase to each sentence below.*

1. My friend loves desert animals. ______________________________

____

2. We visit the Natural History Museum. ______________________________

____

3. The museum has wonderful exhibits. ______________________________

____

4. We get a map when we arrive. ______________________________

____

5. Finally, we find the lizard exhibit. ______________________________

____

6. A plaque describes the snake fossils. ______________________________

____

7. A diagram gives more information. ______________________________

____

8. We spend more than an hour here. ______________________________

____

Look Back

Go back to the prepositional phrases you added.
Circle the preposition in each one.

Unit 4 Review
Lessons 24–34

Adjectives (pp. 112–115) *Underline the adjective(s) in each sentence.*

1. Texas is a large state.

2. It has many famous landmarks.

3. The farmland is rich.

***A, An, The*; Demonstrative Adjectives** (pp. 116–123) *Underline the word in parentheses that correctly completes each sentence.*

4. Dallas is (a, an) city in Texas.

5. We saw (a, an) astronaut in Houston.

6. (This, These) state produces many farm products.

7. (This, These) products include corn, wheat, and other grains.

8. The cotton is harvested by (that, those) workers.

Comparing with Adjectives (pp. 124–127) *Write the form of the adjective in parentheses that correctly completes each sentence.*

9. Only California has a (big) population than Texas. ____________________

10. Gaudalupe Peak is the (high) mountain in Texas. ____________________

11. Dallas is (large) than Austin. ____________________

Comparing with *More* and *Most* (pp. 128–131) *Write **more** or **most** to complete each sentence.*

12. Of the many early Native Americans in Texas, the Caddos were the ____________________ successful farmers.

13. The Jumano people are ____________________ famous for trading than for farming.

14. The Comanche were the ____________________ skillful hunters of all the groups.

Comparing with *Good* and *Bad* (pp. 132–135) *Write the form of the adjective in parentheses that correctly completes each sentence.*

15. The library has many (good) books about Texas. ____________________

16. This encyclopedia has (good) maps than that one. ____________________

17. This book is in the (bad) shape of all the books. ____________________

Adverbs (pp. 136–139) *Underline the adverb in each sentence.*

18. Spanish settlers reached Texas early.

19. They quickly built missions.

20. Texas was part of Mexico then.

Comparing with Adverbs (pp. 140–143) *Write the form of the adverb in parentheses that correctly completes each sentence.*

21. American settlers arrived in Texas (late) than Spanish settlers. ____________________

22. By 1830, Americans were settling Texas (quickly) than Mexicans were. ____________________

23. The American settlers could buy land (cheaply) in Texas than in the United States. ____________________

Using *Good* and *Well*; Negatives (pp. 144–151) *Underline the word in parentheses that correctly completes each sentence.*

24. Settlers came to Texas in search of a (good, well) life.

25. Farmers prepared their new fields (good, well).

26. Many Texans didn't want to be part of Mexico (no more, anymore).

27. No one could (ever, never) find a peaceful solution.

Prepositions and Prepositional Phrases (pp. 152–155) *Underline the prepositional phrase in each sentence. Then circle the preposition.*

28. For years, Texans opposed the Mexican government.

29. Later, Texas became part of the United States.

30. The history of Texas is long and interesting.

Unit 4 Test

DIRECTIONS *Fill in the circle next to the sentence that spells and uses adjectives, adverbs, and negatives correctly.*

1. ○ Sunday was hoter than Saturday.

○ It was the busyest day this year at Greenfield Park.

○ I haven't never seen so many people there.

○ Everyone was having a good time.

2. ○ Those two teams played on a softball field.

○ They played really good.

○ The best of the two teams scored 20 runs.

○ The worst of the two teams scored ten times.

3. ○ There wasn't no more than a light breeze.

○ People could still fly a kites.

○ The box kite flew more gracefully than the hawk kite.

○ A star-shaped kite was the most prettiest.

4. ○ The park has an playground.

○ The merry-go-round was the popularest ride.

○ This line was longer than usual.

○ I didn't bring no money.

5. ○ At the dog run, a beagle was the most calmest dog.

○ An sheepdog did tricks for the crowd.

○ Some dogs behaved good.

○ Some behaved badly.

6. ○ Dad didn't want to get into no rowboat.

○ He never feels well out on the water.

○ I handled the oars gooder this time.

○ I rowed around the lake really good.

7. ○ The swimming pool was the most crowded spot.

○ Mom couldn't find a empty lane.

○ There wasn't no way to swim laps.

○ Going for a swim was the worse decision we made.

8. ○ The park doesn't close until nine o'clock.

○ Usually, we leave much earlyer than that.

○ On Sunday, we weren't in no hurry to leave.

○ We were having a exciting time.

DIRECTIONS *Read the paragraphs, and look carefully at each underlined part. Fill in the circle next to the answer choice that shows the correct use and spelling of adjectives and negatives. If the underlined part is already correct, fill in the circle for "Correct as is."*

Parks are a important part (9) of a community. City parks provide open, green spaces. This spaces provide (10) good places for children and adults to enjoy the outdoors. Without such parks, many people couldn't never play sports (11), exercise outdoors, or have picnics.

State parks are usually far away. Small local parks are easier to reach (12). You can enjoy them anytime with your family and friends. I think our local park is the most friendliest place (13) in the whole neighborhood! It is the best place of all (14) for friends and neighbors to gather.

9.
- ○ a importanter part
- ○ the important part
- ○ an important part
- ○ Correct as is

10.
- ○ These spaces provide
- ○ That spaces provide
- ○ Those space provide
- ○ Correct as is

11.
- ○ could'nt never play sports
- ○ couldn't not play sports
- ○ couldn't ever play sports
- ○ Correct as is

12.
- ○ easyer to reach
- ○ most easy to reach
- ○ more easier to reach
- ○ Correct as is

13.
- ○ a more friendly place
- ○ the friendliest place
- ○ the more friendlier place
- ○ Correct as is

14.
- ○ the good place of all
- ○ the better place of all
- ○ the well place of all
- ○ Correct as is

Lesson 35: Subject Pronouns

LEARN

- A **pronoun** is a word that takes the place of one or more nouns. A **subject pronoun** is used as the subject of a sentence. It tells *whom* or *what* the sentence is about.

  Jason visited Mount Rushmore.
  He photographed the giant sculpture.

  Mr. and Mrs. Gomez went with Jason.
  They enjoyed the trip.

Mount Rushmore

Like nouns, subject pronouns can be singular or plural.

Singular	I	you	he	she	it
Plural	we	you	they		

- A pronoun's **antecedent** is the noun the pronoun refers to. A pronoun and its antecedent must agree in number. If the antecedent is singular, the pronoun must be singular. If the antecendent is plural, the pronoun must be plural. In the first sentence below, the singular pronoun *she* refers to the singular noun *Elena*. In the second sentence, the plural pronoun *they* refers to *Mom and Dad*.

  Elena saw my photographs. **She** saw them yesterday.
  Mom and Dad enjoy traveling. **They** always travel by train.

PRACTICE

A *Write the subject pronoun in each sentence.*

1. I visited Mount Rushmore with my grandmother. ____________

2. She lives in South Dakota. ____________

3. Have you ever been to Mount Rushmore? ____________

4. It shows the giant carved faces of four presidents. ____________

5. They are Washington, Jefferson, Lincoln, and Roosevelt. ____________

6. I also read about Gutzon Borglum. ____________

7. He designed the memorial. ____________

8. Did you know that workers carved with dynamite? ____________

9. They worked for fourteen years. ____________

10. We would like to go back someday. ____________

B *Write the subject pronoun that correctly completes each sentence.*

1. National memorials are places that honor important events.

____________ can be found all over our country.

2. The Wright Brothers National Memorial is in North Carolina.

____________ is a popular place to visit.

3. Orville Wright flew the first airplane.

____________ flew the plane for twelve seconds.

4. Sue visited the Lincoln Boyhood National Memorial in Indiana.

____________ learned that Abraham Lincoln's mother is buried there.

5. Visitors can see the log cabin and barn that sit on the grounds.

____________ can also see a living history demonstration that shows what life was like then.

6. The Franklin Delano Roosevelt Memorial honors our 32nd president.

____________ has four outdoor rooms that trace the history of FDR's four terms in office.

C *Here is an entry from Marsha's journal. Write a subject pronoun from the box to complete each sentence. You will use one pronoun more than once.*

Remember

A **subject pronoun** is used as the subject of a sentence. A pronoun must agree with its antecedent in number.

I	you	he	she	it	we	they

Today, Uncle Jacob and I visited the Lewis and Clark National Historical Park. ______ (1) thought the park was really interesting.

Meriwether Lewis and William Clark were American explorers. ______ (2) traveled across the United States in 1804 and 1805. Their expedition included a young Native American woman named Sacagawea. ______ (3) helped guide the expedition.

In the afternoon, Uncle Jacob and ______ (4) hiked a two-mile trail through the park. There was something really special about this hike. ______ (5) followed the same path that Lewis and Clark took!

Uncle Jacob said historical sites teach you about history firsthand. ______ (6) is right about that!

Did ______ (7) know that the park is in two different states? ______ (8) are Washington and Oregon.

Revising Sentences

WRITE

Additional Resources at grammarworkshop.com

Sometimes you might repeat the same nouns too many times in your sentences.

Keiki went to Philadelphia. Keiki hoped to hear the Liberty Bell, but Keiki was disappointed. The Liberty Bell hasn't rung for more than 160 years.

You can use subject pronouns to replace some of the nouns. That way, your writing will sound smoother and less repetitive. Be sure each pronoun agrees with its antecedent.

Keiki went to Philadelphia. **She** hoped to hear the Liberty Bell, but **she** was disappointed. **It** hasn't rung for more than 160 years.

Liberty Bell

D *Revise the sentences in these passages. Replace some of the nouns with subject pronouns. Watch for pronoun-antecedent agreement.*

1. Darla visited the Benjamin Franklin National Memorial in Philadelphia. Darla was amazed by the statue of Benjamin Franklin. The statue is 20 feet tall and weighs 30 tons. Franklin helped build our country. Franklin was a statesman and a writer. Franklin was also a scientist and inventor.

____

____

____

____

2. The Benjamin Franklin National Memorial holds many of Franklin's possessions. The Benjamin Franklin National Memorial also displays Franklin's early writings. Darla saw a Franklin stove there. Darla also saw the lightning rod that Franklin invented. The lightning rod saved many buildings from fire.

____

____

____

____

Lesson 36: Pronoun-Verb Agreement

LEARN

- In every sentence, the verb must agree with the subject.
  - When the subject pronoun is *he, she,* or *it,* add *-s* or *-es* to the present tense of most action verbs. If the verb ends in *y,* change the *y* to *i* before adding *-es.*

    He hurries to the campsite.
    She pitches the tent.
    It protects the campers from wind and rain.
  - When the subject pronoun is *I, we, you,* or *they,* do not add *-s* or *-es* to the verb.

    I pack everything in my bag.
    We camp all the time.
    You start a campfire.
    They go for a swim.

PRACTICE

A *Write the verb in parentheses that correctly completes each sentence.*

1. I ________________ across the lake with Mom. (paddle, paddles)

2. She ________________ from the canoe. (fish, fishes)

3. We ________________ two fish after a while. (catch, catches)

4. You ________________ to Dan at the tent. (wave, waves)

5. He ________________ to the dock. (rush, rushes)

6. I ________________ back to camp. (race, races)

7. We ________________ a campfire for Mom. (prepare, prepares)

8. She ________________ the fish with Dan. (clean, cleans)

9. They ________________ it over the fire. (fry, fries)

10. It ________________ delicious! (taste, tastes)

B *Write the present tense of the verb in parentheses to correctly complete each sentence.*

1. We ________________ our sleeping bags at sundown. (unroll)

2. You ________________ mosquitoes in the tent. (hear)

3. They ________________ loudly in Dan's ears. (buzz)

4. He ________________ his arms and legs. (scratch)

5. I ________________ all over, too. (itch)

6. He ________________ the flashlight out to Mom. (bring)

7. She ________________ the flashlight on. (switch)

8. It ________________ for three seconds, and then it goes out. (shine)

9. We ________________ lightning in the sky. (see)

10. It ________________ brightly just before the raindrops start. (flash)

11. We ________________ into our sleeping bags. (scurry)

12. They ________________ slightly damp! (feel)

13. I ________________ to get comfortable, but I'm lying on a rock. (try)

14. It ________________ into my back all night. (push)

15. I ________________ we have better luck tomorrow. (hope)

C *Charles wrote this essay about camping. He made seven mistakes in pronoun-verb agreement. Use the proofreading marks in the box to correct the errors.*

Remember

A present-tense verb must agree with the subject pronoun.

Proofreading Marks

^	Add
⊙	Period
ℓ	Take out
≡	Capital letter
/	Small letter

I like camping for many reasons. When you camp, you rely on your own skills to solve problems. Here are some examples. How do you find your way if you get lost in the woods? You uses a compass and a map. What do you do if your tent looks unsteady? You pitches it again and do a better job this time.

Camping also gives you a chance to relax. When my family camps, we leave our digital devices behind. I enjoys the silence, and so does my Mom. She try to write every day. I always carries a few books and spend time reading.

Camping is just plain fun, too. We sings songs and tell stories around the campfire. Mom watches for unusual birds. They flies around our camp sometimes. Other kinds of animals come close, too.

It's true that camping isn't always comfortable. Even so, it makes you feel great!

Look Back Did you correct seven verbs that did not agree with the pronouns?

Write Your Own

WRITE

D *Look at the picture. Then write a sentence to tell what the person or thing named in parentheses is doing. Use a subject pronoun and a present-tense verb in each of your sentences. The first one is done for you.*

1. (the baby ducks) *They swim after their mother.* ______________________

____

2. (the squirrel) ______________________

____

3. (the girl) ______________________

____

4. (the woman and the boy) ______________________

____

5. (the man) ______________________

____

Proofreading Checklist ☑

- ❑ *Did you use subject pronouns for the subjects of your sentences?*
- ❑ *Did you use present-tense verbs?*
- ❑ *Did you check that your subjects and verbs agree?*

Lesson 37: Object Pronouns

LEARN

- An **object pronoun** follows an action verb. It may also follow a word such as *to, in, at, of, with, during,* or *through.*

  I visited **the Washington Monument**.
  I visited **it**.

  Kim joined **my family and me** during our visit.
  Kim joined **us** during our visit.

  I had dinner with **my grandparents** afterwards.
  I had dinner with **them** afterwards.

- These are the object pronouns. Notice that the pronoun *you* can be singular or plural.

Singular	me	you	him	her	it
Plural	us	you	them		

Washington Monument

PRACTICE

A *Write the object pronoun in each sentence.*

1. My grandparents took me to Washington, D.C. ____________
2. A tour guide showed us the sights. ____________
3. "First, I will take you to the National Mall," the guide said. ____________
4. My grandmother asked her about the Washington Monument. ____________
5. Workers finished work on it in 1885. ____________
6. The bus had taken me past many tall buildings. ____________
7. The Washington Monument is the tallest of them all. ____________
8. A glass elevator whisked us to the top of the monument. ____________

9. "The guide will show you the Capitol next," Grandma said. ______

10. "We will see it soon," I answered. ______

B *Read each sentence. Replace the word or words in **boldface** with an object pronoun.*

1. Our nation's lawmakers meet in **the Capitol**. ______
2. Some of **the lawmakers** were at work in the building. ______
3. The Statue of Freedom stands on top of **the dome**. ______
4. I followed **my grandfather** into the Rotunda. ______
5. The huge round room impressed **my grandparents and me**. ______
6. Thousands of people visit **the room** each day. ______
7. I asked **my grandmother** about the large paintings in the Rotunda. ______
8. One of **the paintings** shows the first reading of the Declaration of Independence. ______
9. My grandmother pointed to the **statues of great Americans**. ______
10. We looked closely at **one statue**. ______
11. The person's face was familiar to **my grandmother and me**. ______
12. Since 1986, the Rotunda has been home to this statue of **Dr. Martin Luther King, Jr**. ______

C *Here is a description of a visit to the White House. Write an object pronoun from the box to complete each sentence. You will use some pronouns more than once.*

Remember
An **object pronoun** follows an action verb. It also follows a word such as *to, in, at, of, with, during,* or *through.*

me	you	him	her	it	us	them

"More than a million people come to the White House every year," our guide told ______(1)______ at the start of the tour. It seemed to ______(2)______ that most of ______(3)______ were in our tour group!

"I can only show ______(4)______ 5 of the 132 rooms in the White House," the tour guide explained. "All of ______(5)______ are on the first floor."

The most interesting room to ______(6)______ was the dining room. There are enough tables and chairs in ______(7)______ for 140 dinner guests!

The president works downstairs in the West Wing, but we didn't see ______(8)______. What about the first lady? We didn't see ______(9)______ either.

The living area in the White House is upstairs, but the tour guide couldn't take ______(10)______ there. The only way I'll see that part of the White House is if the country elects ______(11)______ president someday!

Revising Sentences

WRITE

Additional Resources at grammarworkshop.com

Your writing will sound dull if you use the same nouns over and over again.

The Lincoln Memorial honors Abraham Lincoln.
It has a 19-foot statue of Abraham Lincoln inside.

When the overused nouns come after action verbs or after words such as *of* or *to*, you can replace them with object pronouns. Using object pronouns correctly will make your writing clearer and smoother.

The Lincoln Memorial honors Abraham Lincoln.
It has a 19-foot statue of **him** inside.

Lincoln Memorial

D *Revise the second sentence of each pair. Replace an overused noun in the second sentence with an object pronoun.*

1. Take a close look at a penny. The front of the penny shows Lincoln's face, and the back of the penny shows the Lincoln Memorial.

____

____

2. The Lincoln Memorial stands at the end of the National Mall. Many people think the Lincoln Memorial is the most beautiful monument in Washington, D.C.

____

____

3. Lincoln's famous words are carved on the monument. You can read Lincoln's famous words as you walk through the monument.

____

____

4. Lincoln looks sad to some visitors. Other visitors look at Lincoln and say he is smiling slightly.

____

____

Lesson 38: Using *I* and *Me*

LEARN

- **Be careful when you use the pronouns *I* and *me* in sentences. The pronoun *I* is a subject pronoun. *I* is used only as the subject of a sentence.**

  I watch the stars with Adam and Rosa.

The pronoun *me* is an object pronoun. *Me* is used after an action verb or after a word such as *at, for, of, to,* or *with.*

Rosa lends **me** a telescope.
Adam names some stars for **me**.

- **When you speak about yourself and another person, always name the other person first. Then follow the rules above for when to use *I* and *me*.**

  Rosa and I like astronomy.
  Brian shares a telescope with **Rosa and me**.
  At the park, **my friends and I** wait for the nighttime sky.

PRACTICE

A *Write the word or words in parentheses that correctly complete each sentence.*

1. Rosa invited ____________________ to a star-watching party. (Adam and I, Adam and me)

2. She showed ____________________ how to use a telescope. (I, me)

3. ____________________ found the Big Dipper. (I, Me)

4. Adam told ____________________ that there are 100 billion stars in our galaxy. (I, me)

5. ____________________ didn't even know that our sun is a star. (Rosa and I, Me and Rosa)

6. Adam showed ____________________ the star Sirius. (Brian and me, me and Brian)

7. ____________________ were amazed by its brightness! (Brian and I, Brian and me)

8. Brian asked ____________________ why the stars seem to twinkle. (I, me)

9. Adam explained the reason to ________________. (the others and I, the others and me)

10. Now ________________ are fascinated by the stars. (my friends and I, me and my friends)

B *Write **I** or **me** to correctly complete each sentence.*

1. My twin sister Tina and ________________ have a telescope.
2. Uncle George bought it for Tina and ________________ last week.
3. Mom helped ________________ assemble it.
4. My sister and ________________ waited for a clear night.
5. Dad told ________________ that starlight takes millions of years to reach Earth.
6. Tina and ________________ found that hard to believe.
7. Mom pointed out the Great Bear constellation to Tina and ________________.
8. That group of stars didn't look like a bear to ________________.
9. My family and ________________ visited the planetarium yesterday.
10. The guide showed my parents and ________________ a model of the solar system.
11. She told ________________ that the stars shine day and night.
12. Another guide gave ________________ a book about the stars.
13. Both my sister and ________________ learned many facts about outer space.
14. Learning about the stars has also inspired ________________.
15. ________________ wrote a poem called "Starry Day" just yesterday.

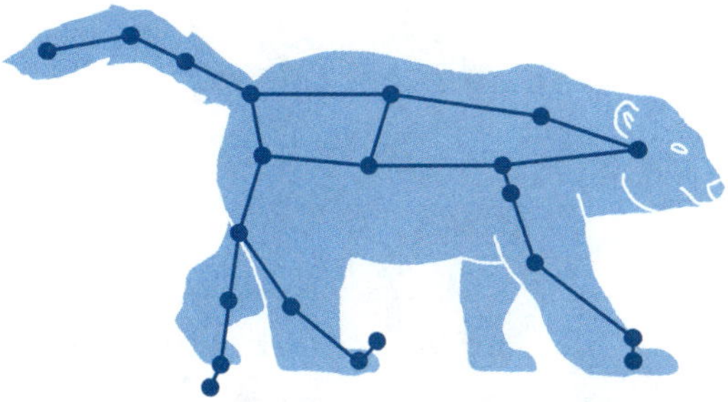

The Great Bear (Ursa Major)

C *Ray wrote this thank-you note to his uncle. He made seven mistakes when using the pronouns* **I** *and* **me**. *Use the proofreading marks in the box to correct the errors.*

Remember

The pronoun *I* is used only as the subject of a sentence. The pronoun *me* is used after an action verb or a word such as *to, for, at,* or *with.*

Dear Uncle George,

Tina and me want to thank you so much for the telescope! Mom helped I set it up last night. You couldn't have gotten me and Tina a better present! Fortunately, the nights are darker here than in most places. The whole family and me can get a great view of the night sky!

Please come visit my family and I soon! Tina and I will show you some stars and planets. Mom has already pointed out two planets, Venus and Mercury. With the telescope, I and Tina hope to spot Jupiter soon.

Thanks again,

Ray

P.S. Me and Tina also are using the sky chart that came with the telescope. It makes everything a lot easier!

Proofreading Marks

^	Add
⊙	Period
ℓ/	Take out
≡	Capital letter
/	Small letter

Look Back **Did you correct seven mistakes with *I* and *me*?**

Additional Resources at grammarworkshop.com

Combining Sentences

WRITE

Pairs of related sentences can sound choppy when you read them. Try combining the sentences into one sentence that expresses the same idea. You can combine the sentences below by joining the noun in the subject of the first sentence and the subject pronoun in the second sentence.

Tina invited Tim to our Planet Watch Party.
I invited Tim to our Planet Watch Party.
Tina **and** I invited Tim to our Planet Watch Party.

Sometimes you can combine related sentences by joining the noun that follows the action verb in the first sentence and the object pronoun in the second sentence.

Tim thanked Tina.
Tim thanked me.
Tim thanked Tina **and** me.

D *Combine each pair of sentences by joining a noun and a pronoun.*

1. Dad showed Tim the planet Venus. I showed Tim the planet Venus.

____

2. Kari lent her binoculars to Luke. Kari lent her binoculars to me.

____

3. Venus looked so bright to Jessie. Venus looked so bright to me.

____

4. Chris tried to find Jupiter. I tried to find Jupiter.

____

5. The planets fascinate my friends. The planets fascinate me.

____

Lesson 39: Possessive Pronouns

LEARN

- A possessive noun shows *who* or *what* has something. A **possessive pronoun** takes the place of a possessive noun.

  Heather's cat is a Siamese.
  Her cat is a Siamese.

- There are two kinds of possessive pronouns. One kind is used before a noun. The possessive pronouns that can be used before a noun are *my, your, his, her, its, our,* and *their*.

  My pet is a tabby cat.
  Your friend has three cats.
  Her cat won a ribbon.
  I love **their** beautiful coats.
  Its gray fur is so soft.
  The cat show was held in **our** town.

The other kind of possessive pronoun is used alone. The possessive pronouns that can stand alone are *mine, yours, his, hers, ours,* and *theirs*.

The Persian cat is **hers**.
The black kitten is **mine**.
His is black, too.
Theirs has white paws.
This one is **ours**.
Where is **yours**?

PRACTICE

A *Underline the possessive pronoun in each sentence. Then write **before a noun** or **used alone** to tell how it is used.*

1. The white cat is mine. ____________
2. Siamese cats are known for their blue eyes. ____________
3. Your cat is a calico. ____________
4. Its coat has black, orange, and white patches. ____________
5. Is this cat carrier yours? ____________
6. Tonya says the Manx cat is hers. ____________
7. Where is its tail? ____________

8. Mr. Kubo brought his cat to the show. ____________________

9. The large Burmese cat is his. ____________________

10. Our cat show will be a great success. ____________________

B *Write the possessive pronoun that correctly completes each sentence.*

1. ____________________ tabby cat has a yellow coat with dark stripes. (Her, Hers)

2. ____________________ cat weighs 23 pounds. (My, Mine)

3. Tails help cats keep ____________________ balance. (their, theirs)

4. One of the winning cats is ____________________. (her, hers)

5. ____________________ hair is short and curly. (It, Its)

6. The longhaired white cat is ____________________. (our, ours)

7. Which cat is ____________________? (your, yours)

8. ____________________ Maine Coon cat is larger than most. (Your, Yours)

9. The 20-year-old cat is ____________________. (my, mine)

10. The final decision is ____________________. (their, theirs)

11. I admire ____________________ independence and curiosity. (it, its)

12. Look at the painting of ____________________ cats. (our, ours)

C *Sue wrote this report about a cat show she went to. She made seven mistakes using possessive pronouns. Use the proofreading marks in the box to correct the mistakes.*

Remember

The possessive pronouns *my, your, his, her, its, our,* and *their* are used before a noun. The possessive pronouns *mine, yours, his, hers, ours,* and *theirs* stand alone.

I have a tabby cat named Ali and a Persian cat named Timtam. Last week, I entered Timtam in a cat show. Timtam is a large male whose fur is long and shiny. Ali is a female, and hers fur has dark stripes. "Ours two cats are beautiful, but Timtam is the more unusual of the two," I told mine mother.

I carried Timtam to the show in a cat carrier. I had lined its sides with light blue silk to make Timtam look even better. At the show, my eyes widened, and mine mouth fell open. I had never seen so many cats!

"Is this cat your?" a judge asked me. "Yes, Timtam is mine," I replied. The judges studied Timtam carefully. Then they moved on to the other cats.

Timtam won a blue ribbon! I laughed and said to Timtam, "This is yours ribbon, but in a way, it's my, too. After all, we worked together to win it!"

Proofreading Marks

^	Add
⊙	Period
ℓ	Take out
≡	Capital letter
/	Small letter

Look Back **Did you correct seven possessive pronouns?**

Write Your Own

WRITE

Additional Resources at grammarworkshop.com

D *Read each short description, and imagine the scene. Then write two sentences to tell more about what is happening. Use a possessive pronoun in each sentence. The first one is done for you.*

1. Two cats are asleep on a sofa.

The cats sleep in their favorite place.

Each cat enjoys its nap.

2. A girl is brushing the long hair of a cat.

____

____

3. Two judges are awarding a ribbon to a prize-winning cat. The cat's owners are standing nearby.

____

____

4. A boy pulls a piece of string to play with a pet cat.

____

____

5. A mother cat washes the small kittens.

____

____

6. A cat watches while a woman opens a can.

____

____

Proofreading Checklist ☑

❑ ***Did you use the correct possessive pronoun in each sentence?***

Lesson 40: Relative Pronouns and Relative Adverbs

LEARN

- In a complex sentence, the second idea is related to the first idea. Sometimes the second idea is introduced by a relative pronoun. The **relative pronoun** relates the two ideas, linking the second idea to a noun in the first idea.

  - Abbey is the girl **who** is on our swim team.
  - She is the person **that** brought the team to victory.
  - The swim cap **which** (or **that**) she lost has red and white stripes.
  - This is the team **whose** coach was honored.
  - He is the coach **whom** we met last year.

When talking about people, use *who, whom,* or *that.* When talking about things, use *that* or *which.* To show who something belongs or relates to, use *whose.*

- Sometimes the **relative adverbs** *where, when,* and *why* introduce the second idea. Use **where** after the word *place* or place words such as *room* or *street*. Use **when** after the word *time* or time words such as *day* or *year*. Use **why** after *reason*.

  - This is the pool **where** the team practices.
  - There was a time **when** we practiced outdoors.
  - There is no reason **why** we can't try again.

PRACTICE

A *Underline the relative pronoun or relative adverb in each sentence.*

1. The swim meet which takes place at our school is always the most thrilling!

2. The swimming events are the only ones that take place indoors.

3. I found the lane where my relay partner was warming up.

4. Angela is the girl with whom I swim in the relay race.

5. There is a good reason why the other team arrived so late.

6. The first race starts at 1 P.M. when everyone is on her mark.

7. The judge who explains the rules was one of the coaches last year.

8. The team that gets the most points will go to the state championships.

9. The team whose mascot is a dolphin won the most medals.

10. We will get our medals tomorrow when we have our team dinner.

B *Write the relative pronoun or relative adverb in parentheses that correctly completes each sentence.*

1. Olympic athletes are the people ________________ I look up to the most. (which, whom)

2. Kim is the girl ________________ parents were both Olympic swimmers. (who, whose)

3. She trains at the sports arena ________________ has an Olympic size swimming pool. (which, who)

4. Roberto is the young man ________________ beat the state record for the 50-meter butterfly. (which, who)

5. The butterfly is a stroke ________________ may seem difficult at first. (that, whom)

6. The lake near my house is ________________ Roberto learned to swim. (when, where)

7. Roberto joined the Men's U.S. Olympic team the year ________________ it won six gold medals. (when, why)

8. His dream of becoming an Olympic champion is the reason

________________ he practices so much. (where, why)

C *Here is a description of a baseball game played at a sports festival. Write a relative pronoun or relative adverb from the box to complete each sentence.*

who	when	whose	why
that	where	which	whom

Remember

Use the relative pronouns *who*, *whom*, or *that* when talking about people. Use *that* or *which* when talking about things. Use *whose* to show who something belongs to. Use the relative adverbs *where* after place words, *when* after time words, and *why* after the word *reason*.

For the first game of the season, the Jonestown Lions played the Smithfield Tigers. The Tigers were the team ________________ won the district championship last year. Its players are the best in the league.

The game started and the Lions were the first to bat. Lucas is the team's star batter ________________ arms are so strong he can knock the ball out of the park. On the first pitch, he hit the ball long and hard. As he slid into home, the umpire called, "Out!"

Lucas asked him for the reason ________________ he had made that call. The umpire said the left fielder had caught the ball the moment ________________ Lucas began his slide into home. Lucas could not believe it.

In disbelief, Lucas went back to the dugout ________________ his team was sitting. It was a call ________________ no one would forget. It was still a close game ________________ ended with the Lions' first win over the Tigers!

Combining Sentences

WRITE

Additional Resources at grammarworkshop.com

You can combine two related sentences with a relative pronoun or relative adverb. When you combine sentences in this way, you avoid repeating words.

The Red Rockets is a soccer team. The soccer team participated in the South Shore tournament.
The Red Rockets is the soccer team **that** participated in the South Shore tournament.

My dad drove me to the soccer field. My team was getting ready for the game there.
My dad drove me to the soccer field **where** my team was getting ready for the game.

D *Read each pair of sentences. Use the relative pronoun or relative adverb in parentheses to combine the sentences. Write the new sentence on the line.*

1. We spotted the player. We admire her the most. (whom) ____________________

____

2. Rachel is the new player. She joined our team last weekend. (who) ____________________

____

3. Mr. Arnold is the coach. His job is to improve our soccer skills. (whose) ____________________

____

4. Dribbling is a skill. It requires a lot of practice. (that) ____________________

____

5. No one knows the reason. The referee cancelled the game. (why) ____________________

____

6. Frosty's is the ice cream shop. My team goes there after every game. (where) ____________________

____

Lesson 41: Contractions with Pronouns

LEARN

- A **contraction** is made by joining two words together. An apostrophe (’) takes the place of any letters that are left out.

Many contractions are formed by joining a pronoun and a verb.

Pronoun and Verb	Contraction	Pronoun and Verb	Contraction
I am	**I’m**	I have	**I’ve**
she is	**she’s**	she has	**she’s**
it is	**it’s**	it has	**it’s**
you are	**you’re**	you have	**you’ve**
they are	**they’re**	they have	**they’ve**
I will	**I’ll**	I had	**I’d**
you will	**you’ll**	you had	**you’d**
we will	**we’ll**	we had	**we’d**
they will	**they’ll**	they had	**they’d**

- Be especially careful when you use the contractions *he’s, she’s,* and *it’s*. The contractions for *he, she,* and *it* and the verbs *is* and *has* are the same.

It is time to go home.
It’s time to go home.

I think **he is** the best writer.
I think **he’s** the best writer.

It has been a busy day.
It’s been a busy day.

We know that **he has** won the prize.
We know that **he’s** won the prize.

PRACTICE

A *Write the contraction for each pair of words.*

1. I am ____________________

2. you will ____________________

3. he is ____________________

4. we are ____________________

5. they had ____________________

6. I have ____________________

PRACTICE A *continued*

7. they are ____________
8. she has ____________
9. we had ____________
10. it has ____________

B *Read each sentence. Replace the pronoun and verb in* ***boldface*** *with a contraction.*

1. **I am** Becky's friend. ____________
2. **You are** Becky's friend, too. ____________
3. **She is** at the National Spelling Bee in Washington, D.C. ____________
4. **We will** meet her at the airport when she returns. ____________
5. **She has** never been to Washington, D.C. ____________
6. **You have** visited many times. ____________
7. **You will** have plenty to talk about. ____________
8. **It is** the day of Becky's flight. ____________
9. **We had** better hurry, or we will be late. ____________
10. I wish **I had** checked the schedule earlier. ____________
11. I hope **she will** arrive late. ____________
12. **It has** taken us an hour to get to the airport. ____________
13. **They are** Becky's mom and dad. ____________
14. I think **he is** Becky's brother. ____________
15. I see that **we are** not late after all. ____________

C *A group of students collected these sayings and bits of advice from their friends and family members. While listing the sayings, they made eight mistakes when using contractions. Use the proofreading marks in the box to correct the errors.*

Remember

An apostrophe (') takes the place of the letter or letters that are left out of a contraction.

- It's called common sense, but its always very rare.
- If you don't believe in something, youll' fall for anything.
- Hed tried to have it both ways and ended up with neither.
- Fish don't get caught if theyve kept their mouths shut.
- We'll have to break some eggs to make an omelet.
- Id rather wear out than rust.
- If you nurse your troubles, theyll only grow larger.
- It's better to give than to receive.
- Your'e going to catch more flies with honey than with vinegar.
- Teach people to fish, and theyr'e fed for a lifetime.

Proofreading Marks

^	Add
⊙	Period
↗	Take out
≡	Capital letter
/	Small letter

Look Back Did you correct eight contractions?

Write Your Own

WRITE

Additional Resources at grammarworkshop.com

D *Imagine that you are writing an ad for a new laundry detergent called Supersuds. Write some sentences that might appear in your ad. In each sentence, include the contraction in parentheses. The first one is done for you.*

1. (it's) *It's the best laundry detergent ever!*

2. (she's) ______________________________

3. (we've) ______________________________

4. (I've) ______________________________

5. (they've) ______________________________

6. (you'll) ______________________________

7. (I'm) ______________________________

8. (you're) ______________________________

Now imagine that you are a scientist writing a review of Supersuds for a newspaper. How might the sentences you write for the review be different from the sentences above? Discuss this question with your classmates.

Proofreading Checklist ☑

- ❑ *Did you use a contraction in each sentence you wrote?*
- ❑ *Did you spell each contraction correctly?*

Unit 5 Review
Lessons 35–41

Subject Pronouns (pp. 160–163) *Write the subject pronoun in each sentence.*

1. I have two friends who are unable to hear. ____________

2. They communicate with American Sign Language. ____________

3. It is also known as ASL. ____________

4. We speak this language together. ____________

Pronoun-Verb Agreement (pp. 164–167) *Underline the verb in parentheses that correctly completes each sentence.*

5. I (practice, practices) the ASL finger alphabet with Terry.

6. We (spell, spells) our names.

7. She (teach, teaches) me with the help of a chart.

8. It (show, shows) all the letters.

Object Pronouns (pp. 168–171) *Write the object pronoun in each sentence.*

9. Sign language helps us in many ways. ____________

10. It helps my friends talk to me. ____________

11. I can tell them jokes using ASL. ____________

12. We wouldn't communicate as well without it. ____________

Using *I* and *Me* (pp. 172–175) *Underline the word or words in parentheses that correctly complete each sentence.*

13. Jim and (I, me) know some Braille.

14. Grandma taught my cousin and (I, me) about this writing system.

15. Grandma showed her Braille writer to (me and Jim, Jim and me).

16. (Jim and I, Jim and me) like to use this machine sometimes.

Possessive Pronouns (pp. 176–179) *Write the possessive pronoun in each sentence.*

17. Louis Braille invented his famous alphabet in 1829. ________________

18. Blind readers use their fingers to read raised dots on paper. ________________

19. Each group of dots has its own meaning. ________________

20. Is this Braille book yours? ________________

Relative Pronouns and Relative Adverbs (pp. 180–183) *Write the relative pronoun or relative adverb in parentheses that correctly completes each sentence.*

21. Mr. Niles is the school custodian ________________ job it is to post all Braille signs. (who, whose)

22. The new elevator at the school is the place ________________ a Braille sign was just posted. (when, where)

23. Our teacher purchased a Braille labeler last year ________________ the class started to learn about Braille. (when, why)

24. Helen Keller is a well-known person ________________ raised money for the blind. (whom, who)

Contractions with Pronouns (pp. 184–187) *Read each sentence. Write a contraction for the pronoun and verb in* ***boldface****.*

25. **They have** put the chart of Braille letters on the wall. ________________

26. **He is** touching the dots with his finger. ________________

27. I think **it is** the letter *a*. ________________

28. **She has** found the dots for the word *hello*. ________________

Unit 5 Test

DIRECTIONS *Fill in the circle next to the sentence that shows the correct spelling and use of pronouns, verbs, adverbs, and contractions.*

1.
- ○ Me and my cousins visit Grandpa every summer.
- ○ We sees something new every time we go there.
- ○ He take us to the aquarium.
- ○ We're amazed by the size of the huge tanks.

2.
- ○ Derek and me hurry to the penguin exhibit.
- ○ It's always been ours favorite.
- ○ "The penguins missed you," Grandpa says.
- ○ "Your favorite visitors are here!" he tell the penguins.

3.
- ○ My cousin Olivia calls to Derek and me.
- ○ Shes' in a hurry to see the walruses.
- ○ "Weve looked at penguins long enough," she says.
- ○ She want to see something else.

4.
- ○ We reads a sign about one walrus.
- ○ Look at the walrus who tusks are 39 inches long.
- ○ It weigh over a ton.
- ○ It's able to float on a chunk of ice.

5.
- ○ Grandpa shows my cousins and I the octopus exhibit.
- ○ He'is as excited as we are.
- ○ I watches the biggest one for a long time.
- ○ It moves its eight arms gracefully.

6.
- ○ "Well visit the sea otters next," Olivia says.
- ○ The otters are cleaning theirs fur.
- ○ We watches them for several minutes.
- ○ Then it's time to move on.

7.
- ○ Me and the others walk through the jellyfish room.
- ○ We talks about their colors and movements.
- ○ My cousins and I are fascinated by them.
- ○ They swims and drifts in their tank.

8.
- ○ We hurries outside to the dolphin area.
- ○ That is the place who we most want to visit.
- ○ They is up to their usual tricks.
- ○ All of us love these amazing mammals.

DIRECTIONS *Read the paragraph, and look carefully at each underlined part. Fill in the circle next to the answer choice that shows the correct use and spelling of pronouns, verbs, and contractions. If the underlined part is already correct, fill in the circle for "Correct as is."*

The dolphins in the show at the aquarium are bottle-nosed dolphins. They're gray in color. Theirs stomachs (9) are a lighter gray, and their backs are a darker gray. One of the dolphins seems to smile at my cousin and me (10). Its not really smiling, but it's mouth (11) looks like a smile. All of a sudden, it leaps out of the water. It snatch (12) a fish from the trainer and swims away. What a show! Youre sure to have the time of your life (13) at the aquarium. My family and me did! (14)

9. ○ They're gray in color. Their stomachs
○ Theyre gray in color. Their stomachs
○ Theyre gray in color. Theirs stomachs
○ Correct as is

10. ○ at me and my cousin
○ at my cousin and I
○ at I and my cousin
○ Correct as is

11. ○ It's not really smiling, but its mouth
○ It's not really smiling, but it's mouth
○ Its not really smiling, but its mouth
○ Correct as is

12. ○ it leap out of the water. It snatch
○ it leaps out of the water. It snatches
○ it leap out of the water. It snatches
○ Correct as is

13. ○ Youre sure to have the time of yours life
○ You're sure to have the time of yours life
○ You're sure to have the time of your life
○ Correct as is

14. ○ Me and my family did
○ I and my family did
○ My family and I did
○ Correct as is

Lesson 42: Writing Sentences Correctly

LEARN

- When you write, you must show where each sentence begins and ends.

Begin every sentence with a capital letter, and end every sentence with a punctuation mark. The end punctuation you use depends on the kind of sentence you write.

Scientist installing part of an earthquake warning system

- End a declarative sentence with a **period (.)**.
  About a million earthquakes occur each year.
- End an interrogative sentence with a **question mark (?)**.
  Are there really that many?
- End an exclamatory sentence with an **exclamation mark (!)**.
  What a huge number that is!
- End an imperative sentence with a **period (.)**.
  Read this article about earthquakes.

- When you rewrite a run-on sentence as two separate sentences, be sure to use capital letters and end punctuation marks correctly.

RUN-ON	Can earthquakes be predicted scientists are working on a warning system.
CORRECTED SENTENCE	Can earthquakes be predicted? Scientists are working on a warning system.

PRACTICE

A *Read each item. Write **correct** or **incorrect** to tell whether the sentence or sentences are written correctly.*

1. Most earthquakes occur under the sea. How lucky that is! ____________

2. Why do you say that ____________

3. most underwater earthquakes are never even noticed ____________

4. Large underwater earthquakes can cause tsunamis
   The results can be very dangerous ____________

5. What is a *tsunami*? It's a Japanese word for a huge wave. ____________

6. all earthquakes occur along fault lines in the earth's crust ____________

7. Have you ever felt an earthquake usually the ground
   shakes gently. ____________

8. Large earthquakes make loud, rumbling noises. ____________

9. most earthquakes last less than a minute ____________

10. Smaller aftershocks can rattle for days afterward. ____________

B *Write these sentences correctly. Use capital letters and the correct end punctuation marks. Write each run-on sentence as two sentences.*

1. scientists use the Richter scale to measure the strength of earthquakes ____________

   ____

2. look at this chart of measurements the scale goes from 0 to 10 ____________

   ____

3. earthquakes below 5 usually don't cause much damage ____________

   ____

4. do you see the 9.5 on the chart ____________

   ____

5. that is the measurement for the biggest earthquake ever the earthquake occurred in

   Chile in 1960 ____________

   ____

C *Melissa wrote this report about the San Francisco earthquake. Four sentences in the report are missing capital letters. Eight sentences are missing end marks. Find the mistakes, and use the proofreading marks in the box to correct them.*

Remember

Begin every sentence with a capital letter. Use the correct end punctuation for each of the four kinds of sentences.

On April 18, 1906, the sun had just risen most people in San Francisco were asleep. Some were getting ready for work.

Suddenly a loud roar filled the air. The ground was shaking, and buildings and power lines were falling. What was happening A huge earthquake was tearing the city apart.

Gas poured out of broken gas lines. Fires broke out everywhere How disastrous they would be Why weren't the fires put out The water lines had broken, too.

After three days, the fires were finally out the shaking had stopped, too. Over 25,000 buildings had fallen. about 490 city blocks had been destroyed.

What lessons did people learn from this disaster? They learned to build stronger buildings they decided to use more flexible pipes, too. What a difference these changes would make in the future

Proofreading Marks

∧	Add
⊙	Period
ℓ/	Take out
≡	Capital letter
/	Small letter

San Francisco, 1906

Look Back Did you correct four mistakes in capitalization and eight mistakes in end punctuation?

Revising Sentences

WRITE

Additional Resources at grammarworkshop.com

D *Read each explanation below about earthquake safety. Then write a statement, command, exclamation, or question you might say to respond to each explanation. The word in parentheses tells you what kind of sentence to write. The first one is done for you.*

1. Earthquakes can be dangerous. Fortunately, there are some important steps you can take to reduce the danger. (question)

What steps can I take to reduce the danger?

____

2. Identify the "danger zones" in your house. These include areas with windows, tall furniture, and heavy objects. These things are dangerous during an earthquake. (exclamation)

____

____

3. You should be aware of safe spots, such as a sturdy desk or table, in a room. They provide cover from falling objects. (question)

____

____

4. If you are outside, move away from tall buildings and power lines. If possible, go to an open space or park. (command)

____

____

5. Most people will never experience a serious earthquake. Still, it's a good idea to be prepared. (statement)

____

____

Lesson 43: Capitalizing Proper Nouns

LEARN

A **proper noun** names a specific person, place, or thing. Each important word in a proper noun begins with a capital letter.

- The names of people, pets, and special groups always begin with a capital letter.
  Darren Smith   Sparky   Little League
- The names of special places begin with a capital letter.
  Elm Street   Overton Park   Canada
  Detroit   New Mexico   Mills Elementary School
- The names of days, months, and holidays begin with a capital letter.
  Tuesday   November   Election Day
- Family titles that refer to specific people begin with a capital letter.
  Grandma   Uncle Dave   Aunt Sue
- Titles of respect that are used with names begin with a capital letter.
  Mr. Luna   Ms. Elkins   Mayor Quinn   President Roosevelt

PRACTICE

A *In each sentence, underline the noun or nouns that should begin with a capital letter. A sentence may have one, two, or three proper nouns.*

1. The last monday in may is memorial day.
2. People from maine to california honor those who gave their lives for our country.
3. The holiday began in 1866 in waterloo, new york.
4. At that time, it was called decoration day.
5. Different states celebrated this holiday in april, may, and june.
6. In 1971, memorial day became a legal holiday throughout the united states.
7. This year, dennis and I marched with the cub scouts in a parade.

8. The parade began at lakehurst elementary school.

9. It ended on main street.

10. Ms. hernandez led the band, and mayor dixon gave a speech.

B *Rewrite each sentence. Capitalize each proper noun correctly.*

1. The fourteenth day of june is called flag day. ______________________

____

2. On that day in 1777, our country's leaders met in philadelphia and adopted the first flag. ______________________

____

3. In 1885, a teacher named bernard cigrand suggested a holiday called flag birthday. ______________________

____

4. President harry truman made flag day an official holiday in 1949. ______________________

____

5. We celebrate a different national holiday in july. ______________________

____

6. The holiday is called independence day. ______________________

____

7. Our country declared its freedom from great britain on july 4, 1776. ______________________

____

C *Mitchell wrote this report about Labor Day. He forgot to capitalize seven proper nouns, and he capitalized one common noun by mistake. Use the proofreading marks in the box to correct the errors.*

Remember

A **proper noun** names a specific person, place, or thing. Begin each important word in a proper noun with a capital letter.

Many holidays honor famous leaders such as abraham Lincoln and Martin Luther King, Jr. The first monday in September, however, honors ordinary working people.

How did this Holiday begin? Two hard-working men get the credit. One was a carpenter in New York. The other was a machine operator in Paterson, new Jersey. Both men wanted everyone to appreciate how hard some people work. In september 1882, they organized a big parade for workers in New York city.

The idea of honoring workers caught on. In 1887, Oregon was the first state to make Labor Day a holiday. In 1894, president Grover Cleveland made it a national holiday. Other countries have similar holidays. In Australia, people celebrate Eight Hour Day. It honors the successful struggle for a shorter working day. In most of the world, a workers' holiday is celebrated on the first day in may.

Proofreading Marks

∧	Add
⊙	Period
ℓ	Take out
≡	Capital letter
/	Small letter

Look Back Did you correct eight mistakes in capitalization?

Write Your Own

WRITE

Additional Resources at grammarworkshop.com

D *Think about the holidays listed below. Write a few sentences to explain why we celebrate each holiday. Tell how you might celebrate the holiday at school or at home. Use proper nouns in your sentences.*

1. Martin Luther King, Jr., Day ______________________________

____

____

____

2. President's Day ______________________________

____

____

____

3. Thanksgiving ______________________________

____

____

____

4. New Year's Eve ______________________________

____

____

____

Proofreading Checklist ☑

❑ *Did you use proper nouns in your sentences?*

❑ *Did you begin each important word in a proper noun with a capital letter?*

Lesson 44: Abbreviations

LEARN

- An **abbreviation** is a short way of writing a word. Many abbreviations begin with a capital letter and end with a period. Here are some of them.

Titles of Respect

Ms. Margaret Wong **Mr.** Alberto Mador **Dr.** Susan Lewis

Addresses

St. (Street) **Ave.** (Avenue) **Rd.** (Road)
Blvd. (Boulevard) **Rte.** (Route) **P.O.** (Post Office)

Months and Days of the Week

May, *June*, and *July* do not have abbreviations.

Jan. Feb. Mar. Apr. Aug. Sept. Oct. Nov. Dec.
Sun. Mon. Tues. Wed. Thurs. Fri. Sat.

- An **initial** is used in place of a name. It is written as a capital letter followed by a period.

Kim Ann Chin **John Edward** Murphy
Kim A. Chin **J. E.** Murphy

- State names that are used with ZIP codes have special two-letter abbreviations. Both letters are capitalized, and no period is used.

AL (Alabama) **CA** (California)

PRACTICE

A *Write each name or abbreviation correctly.*

1. Jan 11 ____________
2. dr ellen rossi ____________
3. 201 Milton ave. ____________
4. Feb 21, 2013 ____________
5. rte. 202 ____________
6. Elm st ____________
7. mon ____________
8. mr L M Kent ____________
9. Oakland, ca ____________
10. PO. Box 112 ____________

B *Read each item below. Follow the directions in parentheses to change it. Use capital letters and periods correctly.*

1. Joan Richards ______________________
(Change the first name to an initial.)

2. 863 Clayton Avenue ______________________
(Use an abbreviation.)

3. 27 Red Rock Boulevard ______________________
(Use an abbreviation.)

4. Saturday, March 5 ______________________
(Use two abbreviations.)

5. Ms. June Marie Garcia ______________________
(Change the first and middle names to initials.)

6. Mobile, Alabama 36601 ______________________
(Use an abbreviation.)

7. Post Office Box 1413 ______________________
(Use an abbreviation.)

8. Closed: Saturday, Sunday, and Monday ______________________
(Use three abbreviations.)

9. 192 Village Road ______________________
(Use an abbreviation.)

10. Doctor Makara Bel Singh ______________________
(Use an abbreviation and two initials.)

Remember

Most abbreviations begin with a capital letter and end with a period.

C *Look at the items below. In each one, some of the abbreviations are written incorrectly. In two of the items, the initials are also written incorrectly. Altogether, there are eleven errors. Use the proofreading marks in the box to correct the errors.*

Proofreading Marks

^	Add
⊙	Period
(Take-out mark)	Take out
≡	Capital letter
/	Small letter

1.

Mr Arthur m. Nagel
41 Hillside ave.
Los Angeles, Ca 90102

2.

Bennett rd.

3.

Jackson Ave

4.

Welcome to the Ellen S King Library
Library Hours: Mon — Thurs. 9–5
fri. — Sat. 9–4
Closed Sun.

5.

Date *Apr 14*

For *Sally*

Josh called.

Message *Don't forget to bring your rock collection to school on tues.*

Look Back Did you correct a total of eleven mistakes?

Write Your Own

WRITE

Additional Resources at grammarworkshop.com

D *Imagine that a cousin named Jackie is visiting you. You took each telephone message described below for her. Fill in the message pad with the missing information. Use abbreviations whenever possible. Part of the first one is done for you.*

1. Doctor Clement's office called on August 24 to ask if Jackie can change her dental appointment from August 31 to September 1 at 10 o'clock.

Date Aug. 24

For Jackie

______________________ called.

Message ______________________

____

____

2. Jackie's friend Anna called on August 25. She wants to know if Jackie can come to a book club meeting this Thursday at 4:30 at the Gomez's house at 240 Kent Road.

Date ______________________

For ______________________

______________________ called.

Message ______________________

____

____

Proofreading Checklist ☑

- ❑ *Did you begin each abbreviation with a capital letter?*
- ❑ *Did you end each abbreviation with a period?*

Lesson 45: Titles

LEARN

- Titles of books, magazines, and newspapers are set off by italics in printed material. When you write by hand, underline these titles.

PRINTED	*Middletown News* (newspaper)
HANDWRITTEN	Middletown News
PRINTED	*James and the Giant Peach* (book)
HANDWRITTEN	James and the Giant Peach

- Titles of songs and most poems are set off by quotation marks.

  "Home on the Range" (song)
  "Casey at the Bat" (poem)
  "The Farmer in the Dell" (song)
  "What Is Pink?" (poem)

- Notice that the first word and each important word in the titles begin with a capital letter. Words such as *a, an, at, and, by, for, in, of, on, the, to,* and *with* are not capitalized unless they are the first or last word in the title.

PRACTICE

A *Write each title correctly.*

1. elmsford journal (newspaper) ______________________
2. highlights for children (magazine) ______________________
3. the sound of music (song) ______________________
4. my side of the mountain (book) ______________________
5. paul revere's ride (poem) ______________________
6. a bicycle built for two (song) ______________________
7. who has seen the wind? (poem) ______________________
8. national geographic for kids (magazine) ______________________

9. the adventures of Tom Sawyer (book) ____________________

10. hudson valley news (newspaper) ____________________

B *Write the title in each sentence on the line. Capitalize each title. Also underline or add quotation marks to set off the title.*

1. I just read this month's sports illustrated for kids. ____________________

____

2. oodles of noodles is a funny poem. ____________________

____

3. We sang I've been working on the railroad in music class. ____________________

____

4. A mouse acts bravely in the book mrs. frisby and the rats of NIMH. ____________________

____

5. If you like funny books about school, read amber brown is not a crayon. ____________________

____

6. your big backyard is a magazine for very young readers. ____________________

____

7. There was an old man with a beard is a short and funny poem. ____________________

____

8. The magazine stone soup publishes stories by children. ____________________

____

9. The fans sang happy days are here again at the end of the game. ____________________

____

C *Alexander wrote this review of the school talent show. He made seven mistakes when writing titles. Use the proofreading marks in the box to correct the errors.*

Remember

Capitalize the first word and each important word in a title. Do not capitalize words such as *a, an, at, and, by, for, in, of, on, the, to,* and *with* unless they begin or end the title.

Did you ever wonder if the students in our school are talented? Last night's talent show proved that we are.

Dylan got the show off to a great start! He played "on the Sunny Side of the Street" on the trumpet. Terry played "Sandpipers on the beach" on the flute. The sad, beautiful sound of her instrument filled the auditorium. Finally, Roxanne's fiddle version of "Turkey In the Straw" had us tapping our feet.

A few students read aloud. Jacob had memorized the poem Stopping by Woods on a Snowy Evening" by Robert Frost. Maya read a funny passage from her favorite book, Alice's Adventures in Wonderland.

The singers were great, too. Patrick sang "Give My Regards To Broadway." Gina also did a great job. She sang "my Favorite Things" while playing a guitar.

All in all, it was a great show. I don't think anyone can say that our students lack talent.

Proofreading Marks

^	Add
⊙	Period
℘	Take out
≡	Capital letter
/	Small letter

Look Back Did you correct seven mistakes in the titles?

Write Your Own

Additional Resources at grammarworkshop.com

WRITE

D *Read each description of a make-believe book, song, or poem. Then make up a title for it. Write your title on the line. The first one is done for you.*

1. a poem about a boy who likes to climb trees with his cat ______

   "Up in the Branches"

2. a song about paddling a canoe on a river ______

3. a magazine for children who like to collect stamps and coins ______

4. a book about two identical twins who play tricks on their classmates ______

5. a poem about the start of a new school year ______

6. a magazine for people who want to help and protect endangered animals ______

7. a song about a big family get-together in the summer ______

8. a book about an immigrant family coming to the United States in 1900 ______

9. a poem about a snowstorm that drops two feet of snow on your neighborhood ______

Proofreading Checklist ☑

- ❑ *Did you begin the first word in each title with a capital letter?*
- ❑ *Did you begin each important word in a title with a capital letter?*

Lesson 46: Commas in a Series

LEARN

A **comma** separates words or ideas in a sentence and tells the reader when to pause.

Sometimes a sentence has a **series**, or list, of three or more items. Use a comma to separate the items in a series.

Our **teachers, parents, and classmates** planned a field day.

The event took place on a **beautiful, warm, sunny** Saturday.

I brought **sunglasses, a hat, and some sunscreen**.

To get to the park, many people **walked, biked, or drove**.

Do not use a comma after the last word in the series.

PRACTICE

A *In each sentence, the items in a series are in* ***boldface****. Add commas to separate the items.*

1. Parents organized **races contests and activities**.
2. People played **softball volleyball and basketball**.
3. I **pitched batted and scored** in the softball game.
4. **Friends relatives and pets** sat nearby and watched us play.
5. **Jess Mario and Kate** hit home runs.
6. For lunch, my Dad grilled the **hamburgers hot dogs and ribs**.
7. I put **lettuce tomato and ketchup** on my hamburger.
8. The ribs tasted **hot spicy and delicious**.
9. Everyone **gnawed nibbled munched and crunched** corn on the cob.
10. For dessert, we ate **big ripe juicy** peaches.

B *Underline the items in a series in each sentence. Then add commas to separate the items.*

1. At the field day, the fishing contest was for parents teachers and students.

2. Blue red and yellow ribbons had been prepared for the winners.

3. I had brought my rod tackle and bait.

4. I hummed whistled and waited for a bite.

5. I caught a small wet wiggly trout right away.

6. It had a blue green and silver back.

7. Next, I hooked two sunfish a catfish and a crab.

8. I threw them back, and they flopped splashed and swam toward the rock.

9. My rod suddenly twitched jerked and pulled.

10. I had hooked a big strong lively bass!

11. I tugged strained and reeled it in.

12. Parents students and the judge gathered around.

13. No one else had caught such a big healthy beautiful bass.

14. I didn't want to carry clean and cook it.

15. Everyone cheered clapped and shouted when I let it go.

C *Paula saw this list of rules at the park. The list contains twelve mistakes in the use of commas in a series. Some commas were left out, and some appear where they don't belong. Use the proofreading marks in the box to correct the errors.*

Remember
Use a comma to separate three or more items in a series.

Proofreading Marks

^	Add
⊙	Period
℘	Take out
≡	Capital letter
/	Small letter

PARK RULES

- The trees shrubs and wildflowers in this park are protected. Visitors should not cut, damage or remove any plant.
- The hunting trapping or harming of animals is forbidden. Fishing in the pond and streams is permitted.
- Walking jogging, and bicycling are permitted, on park trails.
- Horseback riding is permitted on marked trails. Visitors should not lead, ride or walk a horse in other areas of the park.
- No one is permitted to sell, food, drinks, or other items in the park.
- Park fireplaces stoves and grills may be used in picnic areas. No one is permitted to light build, or maintain a fire in other areas of the park.

Look Back Did you correct twelve mistakes in the use of commas in a series?

Combining Sentences

WRITE

Additional Resources at grammarworkshop.com

Sometimes you can use a series to combine short, choppy sentences to make your writing smoother. The underlined words in each sentence below tell what games the children played. You can put the words in a series to make one smooth sentence.

The young children played tag.
They played hopscotch.
They played dodgeball.

The young children played tag, hopscotch, **and** dodgeball.

You can also put groups of words in a series.

The parents grilled hamburgers.
They made fruit salad.
The parents poured water for everyone.

The parents grilled hamburgers, made fruit salad, **and** poured water for everyone.

D *Rewrite the underlined sentences in this journal entry on the lines below. Combine each group of underlined sentences into one sentence by using a series.*

I wasn't looking forward to the class trip to the park. Now I'm glad I went. The trip was fun. It was interesting. The trip was educational.

I liked the nature walk best. Along the way, I saw a red-tailed hawk. I saw a Baltimore oriole. I saw a scarlet tanager. I was also surprised by how many different trees grow in the park. Chestnut trees grow in the park. Walnut trees grow there. Pecan trees grow in the park, too.

Back at the picnic tables, we had some more fun. Everyone gathered around Ms. Grady, our teacher. Ms. Grady handed out songbooks. She played the guitar. She led a sing-along. What a great way to end the day!

Lesson 47: More Commas

LEARN

Here are some more uses for commas.

- Use a comma to set off an introductory word such as *yes, no,* or *well* from the rest of a sentence.
  Yes, I have some silly riddles to tell.
  No, not everyone likes them.
  Well, I think they're funny.

- Use a comma or commas to set off the name of a person being spoken to.
  - If the name is at the beginning of the sentence, place a comma after the name.
    Todd, what gets wet the more you dry?
  - If the name is at the end of the sentence, place a comma before the name.
    I don't know**, Ellen.**
  - If the name is in the middle of the sentence, place commas before and after the name.
    The answer**, Todd,** is a bath towel!

PRACTICE

A *Read each sentence. Write* **introductory word** *or* **name of person spoken to** *in order to tell what words are set off by the comma or commas.*

1. Michelle, do you know what gets bigger the more you take away from it? ________________
2. No, I can't imagine what it could be. ________________
3. The answer, Michelle, is a hole in the ground. ________________
4. What crosses the country without moving, Tino? ________________
5. Jodi, is this another silly riddle? ________________
6. Yes, and the answer is a superhighway. ________________

7. Avi, what breaks whenever you say it? ____________________

8. Hmm, I have no idea. ____________________

9. I think, Brenda, that the answer is "silence." ____________________

10. That is the correct answer, Tom! ____________________

B *In each sentence, add commas where they are needed. The first one is done for you.*

1. Do you know a place Bob where you can always find happiness?
2. Well let me think about that.
3. Ray is the answer "the dictionary"?
4. Yes you got it!
5. What coat is always wet when you put it on Nancy?
6. Hmm I think it's a coat of paint.
7. What is lighter than a feather Sandy but harder to hold?
8. Hmm could it be "a thought"?
9. No the answer is "your breath"!
10. Okay I have one for you.
11. Pam what's the difference between the North Pole and the South Pole?
12. It's all the difference in the world Ben!
13. You've heard Terri that two's company and three's a crowd.
14. Well do you know what four and five are?
15. Yes I know that four and five are nine!

C *Leanne left out nine commas in the script that she wrote for the class comedy show. Find the mistakes, and use the proofreading marks in the box to correct the errors.*

Remember

Use a comma after introductory words such as *yes* and *no*. Also, use a comma to set off the name of a person being spoken to.

Leanne	Akira, I hear things are looking up for your mom at work.
Akira	Yes, that's true. She just got a job as an astronomer.
Jamie	Hmm I thought she was a weather forecaster on TV Akira.
Akira	No not anymore Jamie. The weather here never agreed with her!
Jamie	Guys, my poor dad finds things really dull at his job.
Leanne	What kind of work does he do Jamie?
Jamie	Oh, he's a knife sharpener.
Leanne	My dad is a jeweler. He sells watches all day.
Akira	That's funny Leanne. My uncle watches cells all day. He works in a biology laboratory.
Jamie	I hear, Akira that you want to be a pilot someday.
Akira	Yes it's the type of job in which you can go really far! What about you, Jamie?
Jamie	Well I'm thinking about becoming a roofer. That way, I can go straight to the top!

Proofreading Marks

^	Add
⊙	Period
ℓ/	Take out
≡	Capital letter
/	Small letter

Look Back Did you add nine missing commas?

Write Your Own

WRITE

Additional Resources at grammarworkshop.com

D *On the lines below, write your own funny script that shows a conversation between you and one or two friends. You can use jokes you know or a funny conversation you have heard for ideas. In your script, use introductory words and the names of people being spoken to. Use the script on page 214 as a model.*

1. ______________ ______________________________

____

____

2. ______________ ______________________________

____

____

3. ______________ ______________________________

____

____

4. ______________ ______________________________

____

____

5. ______________ ______________________________

____

____

Proofreading Checklist ☑

- ❑ *Did you use commas after introductory words such as* ***yes, no,*** *and* ***well?***
- ❑ *Did you use commas to set off the names of people being spoken to?*

Lesson 48: Parts of a Letter

LEARN

- A **friendly letter** is written to someone you know well. In a friendly letter, the **greeting** and **closing** begin with a capital letter and end with a comma. Commas are also used in the **heading** to separate the city and state and to separate the day and year.

9 Pine Street Pittsburgh, PA 15211 May 7, 2013	**heading**
Dear Joan,	**greeting**
Our new swimming pool is almost ready. Bring your bathing suit when you visit us in July.	**body**
Your friend,	**closing**
Margaret	**signature**

- A **business letter** is usually written to someone you don't know. In a business letter, include an **inside address** that gives the name and address of the person you are writing to. Use a **colon (:)** after the **greeting**. You will also need to sign and print your name.

9 Pine Street Pittsburgh, PA 15211 May 10, 2013	**heading**
Mr. John Johnson Johnson Pool Products 15 Spring Street Madison, WI 53703	**inside address**
Dear Mr. Johnson:	**greeting**
Please mail me your catalog of pool games and swimming accessories. I am especially interested in diving masks and snorkel sets.	**body**
Yours truly,	**closing**
Margaret Richards	**signature**
Margaret Richards	

PRACTICE

A *Write each letter part correctly.*

1. June, 17 2013 ____________

2. Akron OH, 44319 ____________

3. dear kenny ____________

4. your Friend ____________

5. dear Ms. Cahill ____________

6. 21 fox lane ____________

B *Complete the letter with the missing letter part.*
Write the letter part correctly.

Gillette NJ 07933	184 ridge Road
your friend	dear margaret

____

____

June 15, 2013

____

I'm sorry to hear about the leak in your new pool. I hope the pool company can fix it soon. I know the whole family is looking forward to using it this summer.

I can't wait to see you in July. We have so much to catch up on.

____

Joan

C *Margaret wrote this letter. In all, she made six mistakes in the use of capitalization and punctuation. Use the proofreading marks in the box to correct the errors.*

Remember
Use a comma after the greeting in a friendly letter. Use a colon after the greeting in a business letter.

Proofreading Marks

^	Add
⊙	Period
ℓ	Take out
≡	Capital letter
/	Small letter

9 Pine Street
Pittsburgh, pa 15211
June 28 2013

Ms. Tonya Ruiz
Community Park Recreation Center
111 Kensington Avenue
Pittsburgh PA 15211

Dear Ms. Ruiz

I heard that you will be offering swimming lessons for children under the age of 12 this summer. I am very interested in your swimming program. Please send me a schedule for these lessons.

sincerely Yours,
Margaret Richards
Margaret Richards

Look Back Did you correct six mistakes in capitalization and punctuation?

Write Your Own

WRITE

Additional Resources at grammarworkshop.com

D *Write a friendly letter or a business letter. If you write a friendly letter, tell a friend or relative what you like most about school this year. If you write a business letter, make a suggestion to the principal of your school for a program or activity that your school might offer.*

Proofreading Checklist ☑

- ❑ *Did you use commas and capital letters correctly in your letter?*
- ❑ *Did you use a comma after the greeting if you wrote a friendly letter?*
- ❑ *Did you use a colon after the greeting if you wrote a business letter?*

Lesson 49: Quotations

LEARN

- A **quotation** is a speaker's or writer's exact words. Follow these rules when writing quotations.
  - Use quotation marks in *dialogue* or to set off a speaker's or writer's exact words. Always capitalize the first word of a quotation.
    Nancy said, **"L**ittle inventions make life easier."
  - When a quotation comes at the end of a sentence, use a comma before the quotation to separate it from the words that name the speaker or writer. Put the end mark inside the quotation marks.
    Cy exclaimed**,** "How clever some inventors are**!**"
  - When a quotation that is a statement or command comes at the beginning of a sentence, put a comma inside the closing quotation marks.
    "Harvey Kennedy invented shoelaces**,**" Nancy said.
    "Try living without them**,**" she added.
  - If the quotation is a question or an exclamation, put the question mark or the exclamation mark inside the closing quotation marks.
    "Who invented the toothpaste tube**?**" Liam asked.
    "What a great invention that was**!**" I exclaimed.
- Do not use quotation marks when you do not use a speaker's or writer's exact words.
  Nancy said, "Let's look up the inventor's name."
  Nancy said that we should look up the inventor's name.

PRACTICE

A *Put quotation marks around each speaker's or writer's exact words. If the sentence does not give the exact words, do not add quotation marks.*

1. Terry claimed that the best inventions are very simple.

2. Liam said, Look at this picture of Benjamin Franklin.

3. He invented the lightning rod! Liam shouted.

4. How did he get the idea for it? Amy asked.

5. Liam said that Franklin wanted to protect buildings from lightning.

6. Mei said, Here's a picture of the first paper clip.

7. I asked, When was it invented?

8. It was invented in 1899 in Norway, Mei replied.

9. Nancy added that paper clips, tape, and ballpoint pens were all great inventions.

10. Where would we be without them? she asked.

B *Rewrite each sentence that is incorrectly written. Use quotation marks, capital letters, and punctuation marks correctly. If a sentence is correct as is, write* ***correct****.*

1. The traffic light was invented in 1923 Liam said. ______________________

____

2. Who invented it asked Mei. ______________________

____

3. Liam replied that the inventor was Garrett Morgan. ______________________

____

4. Nancy said here's an 1883 picture of the first zipper. ______________________

____

5. Terry asked how did it get its name? ______________________

____

6. Nancy explained that the invention made a *z-z-zip* sound. ______________________

____

C *Read the conversation below. In it, there are nine mistakes in the use of capital letters, commas, quotation marks, and end marks. Use the proofreading marks in the box to correct the errors.*

Remember
Use quotation marks around the exact words of a speaker.

Terry asked "Are all inventors geniuses?"

Amy responded, "no, I don't think so." She added that some inventors just see a need for a new product and work hard to fill it.

"Other inventors have a sudden, bright idea," Mei added.

"According to this book, some important inventions were accidents" Nancy exclaimed.

Cy remarked, I once had a good idea for making adjustable training wheels for my bike"

Terry asked, "Did you do anything with your idea?

"No, I wasn't sure how to go about it" Cy replied.

Nancy said, "I'd like to be an inventor someday."

Mei said, "there's no time like the present."

"What do you mean" asked Nancy.

"I mean we could form our own club for young inventors," Mei responded.

Proofreading Marks

∧	Add
⊙	Period
℘	Take out
≡	Capital letter
/	Small letter

Look Back **Did you correct nine mistakes in punctuation and capitalization?**

Write Your Own

Additional Resources at grammarworkshop.com

WRITE

D *Imagine you are one of the students in the conversations below. Join each conversation by asking a question, making a statement, giving a command, or uttering an exclamation. Use quotation marks to set off your words.*

Conversation 1

"I have a great idea for an invention," Terry said.

"It's an electric sweater," she added.

"How would it work?" asked Cy.

"A battery would warm up the wires in the sleeves," Terry replied.

"I don't think that's very practical!" Liam exclaimed.

___

___

___

Conversation 2

"Inventors need to patent their inventions," said Mr. Rossi, a local inventor.

"What's a patent?" Liam asked.

"It protects an inventor's ideas," Mei explained.

"It also makes it possible for an inventor to earn money from an invention," Mr. Rossi added.

___

___

___

Proofreading Checklist ☑

- ❑ *Did you set off your words with quotation marks?*
- ❑ *Did you use capital letters, commas, quotation marks, and end marks correctly?*

Lesson 50: Words Often Misspelled

LEARN

- **Homophones** are words that sound the same but have different spellings and meanings. Some homophones are possessive pronouns, such as *their*, and others are contractions, such as *they're*. Think about the meaning of the word to help you choose the correct spelling.

Homophone	Meaning	Sentence
there	in that place	**There** are many books about Ramona.
they're	they are	**They're** favorites of mine.
their	belonging to them	**Their** illustrations are funny.
it's	it is (*or* it has)	**It's** the funniest story I have ever read.
its	belonging to a thing	**Its** main character is Ramona Quimby.
you're	you are	**You're** going to love *Ramona Forever*.
your	belonging to you	You can borrow a copy from **your** library.
to	preposition	Return the book **to** the library.
two	the sum of 1 and 1	I read *Beezus and Ramona* **two** times.
too	also	I enjoyed that book, **too**.
tale	a story	*Ramona's World* is a good **tale**.
tail	the back part of an animal	Ribsy the dog wagged its **tail**.
right	correct	These hilarious stories are **right** for you.
write	create a story	The author can **write** a good tale.

- **When unsure which spelling is correct, use a dictionary.**

PRACTICE

A *Write the meaning of each homophone. Then write* **contraction** *if the homophone is a contraction. Write* **possessive pronoun** *if it is a possessive pronoun. If it is neither, write* **neither**. *The first one is done for you.*

1. their ___belonging to them___ ___possessive pronoun___

2. they're ________________ ________________

3. there ________________ ________________

4. its ____________________ ____________________

5. right ____________________ ____________________

6. you're ____________________ ____________________

7. tail ____________________ ____________________

8. too ____________________ ____________________

B *Write the homophone in parentheses that correctly completes each sentence.*

1. Will you bring your copy of *Ramona's World* ____________________ school? (to, too)

2. ____________________ a popular book among young readers. (Its, It's)

3. Beverly Cleary is ____________________ author. (its, it's)

4. She grew up in Oregon, and her stories are set ____________________. (their, there)

5. I have read ____________________ of her books. (two, too)

6. You are ____________________ about her books. (right, write)

7. It may even make you want to ____________________ your own Ramona adventure. (right, write)

8. You might enjoy a book called *Henry and Ribsy,* ____________________. (to, too)

9. It is a ____________________ about Henry Huggins and his dog Ribsy. (tale, tail)

10. ____________________ neighborhood was once a quiet place. (There, Their)

11. ____________________ up to Henry and Ribsy to change that! (Its, It's)

12. ____________________ sure to love Beverly Cleary's books. (Your, You're)

C *Maria wrote this book report. She made six mistakes when using homophones. Use the proofreading marks in the box to correct the errors.*

Remember
When using homophones, pay attention to the way they are used. For example, *they're, it's,* and *you're* are contractions, while *their, its,* and *your* are possessive pronouns that show ownership.

Proofreading Marks

^	Add
⊙	Period
(delete mark)	Take out
≡	Capital letter
/	Small letter

Ramona's World by Beverly Cleary is a very funny book. Its a story about the kind of everyday events all of us can recognize. There told in such a humorous way that they cause everyone too laugh.

When the book begins, it is the first day of school. Ramona is looking forward to an exciting year, but there are a few problems, two. Ramona's teacher likes her first essay, but it's filled with misspelled words. When the teacher begins to right the mistakes on the board, Ramona is horrified.

On the bright side, Ramona and Daisy Kidd become friends. One day, they're playing in an upstairs crawl space. Its floor is only a layer of plaster, and Ramona's legs break through the attic. Is she hurt? Are you curious? Read the book. Your sure to enjoy it.

Look Back **Did you correct six spelling mistakes?**

Write Your Own

WRITE

Additional Resources at grammarworkshop.com

D *Write a short book report about a book you've enjoyed recently. Be sure to give the title and author of the book. Then give your opinion about the book. Tell why you think your classmates might enjoy the book, too. Use some of the homophones below in your report.*

it's	its	you're	your	they're
there	their	to	too	two
right	write	tail	tale	

Proofreading Checklist ☑

- ❑ *Did you use some of the homophones in your report?*
- ❑ *Did you spell each homophone correctly?*

Lesson 51: Words Often Confused

LEARN

- When two words sound alike or are similar in spelling, the two words can be confused. For example, the word *advice* is often confused with the word *advise*. To avoid confusion, learn the meaning and spelling of each word. *Advice* is helpful information you give to someone. When you *advise* someone, you give him or her a helpful suggestion.

  Our teacher gave us **advice** on ways to prepare for test day.
  He said, "I **advise** you all to stop studying tonight and to sleep well."

- If you are unsure of which word to use, you can use a dictionary.

PRACTICE

A *Match each word in Column A to its meaning in Column B. Write the letter of the correct meaning on the line. If you are unsure of the meaning, check a dictionary.*

	A	*B*
____	**1.** desert	**a.** the star that Earth revolves around
____	**2.** proof	**b.** more distant
____	**3.** all ready	**c.** to show that something is true
____	**4.** further	**d.** dry, sandy land
____	**5.** sun	**e.** a male child
____	**6.** by	**f.** in addition to something
____	**7.** prove	**g.** by this time
____	**8.** dessert	**h.** a sweet food served at the end of a meal
____	**9.** farther	**i.** preposition that tells who/what did the action
____	**10.** already	**j.** completely ready

PRACTICE A *continued*

____ **11.** buy **k.** to get something by paying for it with money

____ **12.** son **l.** evidence

B *Write the word in parentheses that correctly completes each sentence.*

1. Today, we had to write our favorite ________________ recipes. (desert, dessert)

2. My favorite recipe for lemon cookies was given to me ________________ my great grandmother. (buy, by)

3. The first step in my recipe is to ________________ all the ingredients. (buy, by)

4. When mixing the batter, I would ________________ everyone to use a wooden spoon. (advice, advise)

5. If you want to go a step ________________, try making a lemon frosting. (farther, further)

6. Today, a guest chef and his ________________ came to our school. (sun, son)

7. They gave our class ________________ on how to bake bread. (advice, advise)

8. They said that the ________________ of a good baker is "in the pudding." (prove, proof)

9. It was ________________ time for lunch when the chef took fresh baked bread out of the oven. (all ready, already)

10. I took a loaf of bread home to ________________ to my family that I am now a real baker! (proof, prove)

C *Raj wrote this journal entry about his art class. He made six mistakes when writing words that are often confused. Find the mistakes, and use the proofreading marks in the box to correct the errors.*

Remember
Use the word with the intended meaning. Spell the word carefully.

Today in art class, our teacher, Ms. Nova, described a scene and asked us to paint it. Before we started, we each got a piece of paper and some paints. When we were already, she started to read the description.

Ms. Nova talked about cactuses, sand, and tumbleweed. That's when I knew she was describing a dessert. I quickly picked up my pencil and started drawing. Then I used watercolors to fill in my drawing. I had a few green cactus plants in front. Further away were sandy, brown hills. Beyond this, I could think of nothing farther to draw! That's when I asked Ms. Nova for advise. She told me to close my eyes and imagine the picture again. When I opened my eyes, I knew just what to add. I drew a bright, orange son, a scaly iguana, and a flying eagle that soared through the air. I was so happy with my colorful desert scene that I couldn't wait to take it home!

Proofreading Marks

^	Add
⊙	Period
℘	Take out
≡	Capital letter
/	Small letter

Look Back Did you use the correct meaning of six words that are often confused?

Write Your Own

WRITE

Additional Resources at grammarworkshop.com

D *Write sentences about how to make or do something. Use the word in parentheses in each sentence.*

1. (already) ______________________________

____

2. (advice) ______________________________

____

3. (sun) ______________________________

____

4. (proof) ______________________________

____

5. (buy) ______________________________

____

6. (further) ______________________________

____

7. (all ready) ______________________________

____

8. (prove) ______________________________

____

Proofreading Checklist ☑

❑ *Did you use each word in parentheses correctly?*

Unit 6 Review
Lessons 42–51

Writing Sentences Correctly (pp. 192–195) *Write each sentence correctly. Write each run-on sentence as two sentences.*

1. what sorts of things do you collect

____

2. we have many cards we trade them sometimes

____

3. what a great collection you have

____

Capitalizing Proper Nouns (pp. 196–199) *Read each sentence. Write each proper noun correctly.*

4. My aunt lives near golden gate park. ____________

5. We visited her on the fourth of july. ____________

6. I gave aunt betty a small figurine of a cat. ____________

Abbreviations (pp. 200–203) *Write each name or abbreviation correctly.*

7. dr Vivian Hayes ____________

8. thurs ____________

9. mr Donald a Banks ____________

10. p o Box 124 ____________

Titles (pp. 204–207) *Write each title correctly.*

11. the mouse and the motorcycle (book) ____________

12. a day at the beach (poem) ____________

13. sports illustrated for kids (magazine) ____________

Commas (pp. 208–215) *In each sentence, add commas where they are needed.*

14. My mother father and brother all collect things.

15. Mom do you collect old maps?

Parts of a Letter (pp. 216–219) *Write each letter part correctly.*

16. dear Charlie ______________________________

17. sincerely yours ______________________________

18. Baltimore MD 21202 ______________________________

19. dear Mayor Hanks ______________________________

Quotations (pp. 220–223) *Add commas and quotation marks where necessary to show each speaker's words.*

20. Claire said Everyone in my family collects something except me.

21. Mimi asked How many miniature horses do you have on your dresser?

22. I guess I have a collection after all! Claire laughed.

Words Often Misspelled (pp. 224–227) *Underline the homophone in parentheses that correctly completes each sentence.*

23. (Their, There) will be a doll auction this weekend.

24. Mia's cousin likes to attend doll auctions, (to, too).

25. (Your, You're) favorite hobby is collecting art.

26. (Its, It's) a family tradition to go to auctions every spring break.

Words Often Confused (pp. 228–231) *Underline the word in parentheses that correctly completes each sentence.*

27. A furniture collector can (prove, proof) that Fran's chair is worth a lot of money.

28. At the auction, her chair is (farther, further) down the aisle.

29. To get (advise, advice) on collecting comics, Mike spoke to an expert.

30. The annual auction was (already, all ready) closed to the public.

Unit 6 Test

DIRECTIONS *Fill in the circle next to the sentence that shows the correct use of commas, capital letters, end marks, spelling, and quotation marks.*

1.
- ○ This summer, I went to day Camp.
- ○ I went from july 15 to august 12.
- ○ Dad drove to the Jackson Recreation Center, too.
- ○ He took Hyland road to Oak avenue.

2.
- ○ What did I like most about camp.
- ○ Well, the counselors gave really good advice.
- ○ We played basketball soccer, and tennis.
- ○ We wrote practiced and performed our own plays.

3.
- ○ The camp director was Ed I Fox.
- ○ What a great camp director he is?
- ○ "Let's have another great day! he told us every morning.
- ○ He kept everyone safe, happy, and busy.

4.
- ○ Ms. Tonya Gray wants prove that we are good swimmers.
- ○ "Anyone can learn to swim," she said.
- ○ She took us to the pool at hillsdale Park, too.
- ○ We also took day trips to the zoo the museum, and a baseball game.

5.
- ○ We had a sing-along every Friday.
- ○ Mr Fox played "You Are My Sunshine" on his guitar.
- ○ I sang "I'm Sitting On Top Of The World" for everyone.
- ○ "You sing well", they told me.

6.
- ○ Would you be surprised to hear that we read each day.
- ○ Ms. Nieves said "Reading will help you be ready for school."
- ○ "You can also read just for the fun of it" she added.
- ○ We traded books every Wednesday.

7.
- ○ Some campers also go to south valley school.
- ○ I will look for them this fall
- ○ "We didn't know you last year." they told me.
- ○ "We will now be friends at school," I replied.

8.
- ○ Robert, do you want to go to camp next summer.
- ○ Yes I'd love to!
- ○ Friends, counselors, and teachers made camp special.
- ○ I want to spend July and August at green valley park!

DIRECTIONS *Read the letter, and look carefully at each underlined part. Fill in the circle next to the answer choice that shows the correct use of commas, capital letters, end marks, and quotation marks. If the underlined part is already correct, fill in the circle for "Correct as is."*

199 Crestview Avenue
Little York, IN 47139
September 14 2013
(9)

dear mr Fox
(10)

I'm back in school from Monday to friday, and Summer is over. (11) Still, I think about day camp at Green Valley Park. What a great experience it was!

I told my friend Ed about camp. Now he says, "next year, I'll go with you". (12) I know he'll love the lessons, activities, and trips. (13) Thank you for everything.

yours truly
(14)
Robert Walker

9. ○ September, 14 2013
○ September 14, 2013
○ september 14, 2013
○ Correct as is

10. ○ dear Mr Fox
○ Dear Mr. Fox
○ Dear Mr. Fox,
○ Correct as is

11. ○ friday, and summer is over.
○ Friday, and summer is over.
○ Friday. And Summer is over
○ Correct as is

12. ○ "Next year, I'll go with you."
○ "Next year, I'll go with you".
○ "next year, I'll go with you."
○ Correct as is

13. ○ lessons activities and trips
○ lessons, activities and trips,
○ lessons, activities, and trips,
○ Correct as is

14. ○ Yours truly
○ Yours Truly
○ Yours truly,
○ Correct as is

INDEX

A

A, an, the, 116–119
defined, 116
with singular and plural nouns, 116, 118
in titles, 204, 206

Abbreviations, 200–203
and capitalization in, 196, 200, 202
defined, 200
and periods in, 200, 202

Action verbs, 60–63
defined, 60
and past tense of, 72
with pronouns, 164, 166, 168, 170, 171, 172, 174

Addresses
abbreviations in, 200
in letters, 216

Adjectives, 112–115. See also *A*, *an*, *the*; *More*, *most*, and spelling rules
combining sentences with, 115
in comparisons, 124–127
defined, 112, 114
demonstrative, 120–123
good and *bad* as, 132–135
good vs. *well*, 144–147
order of, 112–115
with linking verb *be*, 112
with nouns, 112, 114, 144, 146
spelling rules for, 124, 126, 128, 130

Adverbs, 136–139, 140–143
comparing with, 140–143
defined, 136, 138
list of, 136
spelling rules for, 136, 140, 142
and verbs, 136, 138, 144, 146
well vs. *good*, 144–147

Agreement
pronoun-verb, 64, 68, 80, 88, 90, 164–167
subject-verb, 64, 66, 68, 70, 80, 82, 88, 90

And
capitalization rule for, 202, 206
to combine sentences with, 19, 23, 24, 26, 27, 32, 47, 71, 175, 211
in compound sentences, 24, 26, 27
as coordinating conjunction, 24–27
correcting run-on sentences with, 32
with series, 211

Antecedents. *See* Pronouns and antecedent agreement

Apostrophes
in contractions, 104, 106, 184, 186
in possessive nouns, 52

Articles. See *A*, *an*, *the*

Audience, 219, 227

B

***Bad*, in comparisons**, 132–135

Be
in contractions, 104, 184
as helping verb, 84
as linking verb, 80–83
and subject-verb agreement, 80, 82
and tenses of, 80

Better*, *best. See *Bad*, in comparisons

Bodies. *See* Letters, parts of

Book titles. See *A*, *an*, *the*, in titles; Capitalization, in titles; Italics, in titles

Business letters, 216, 218. *See also* Letters,
colons in, 216, 218
defined, 216

But
to combine sentences with, 24, 26, 27
in compound sentences, 24, 26, 27
as coordinating conjunction, 24–27

C

Capitalization
in abbreviations, 196, 200, 202
of calendar dates, 196
in letters, 216
of names, 196
of proper nouns, 40, 42, 196, 198
in quotations, 220
in sentences, 8, 192, 194
in titles, 204, 206
in titles of respect, 196

Closings. *See* Letters, capitalization in, commas in, parts of

Colons, in letters, 216, 218

Combining Sentences, 19, 23, 27, 47, 71, 115, 183
with *and*, *but*, or *or*, 19, 23, 24, 26, 27, 32, 47, 71, 175, 211
and commas, 24
and run-ons, 32

Commands. *See* Imperative sentences

Commas
in compound sentences, 24
with conjunctions, 24
after introductory words in sentences, 212, 214
in letters, 216, 218
in quotations, 220
in series, 208–211

Common nouns, 40–43
defined, 40

Comparisons
with adjectives, 124–127, 132–135
with adverbs, 140–143
with *good* and *bad*, 132–135
with *good* vs. *well*, 144–147
with *more* and *most*, 128, 130, 140, 142

Complete predicates, 12, 14, 16, 20, 22
defined, 12, 14

Complete subjects, 12, 14, 16, 18, 20
defined, 12, 14

Complex sentences, 28–31
and commas in, 28
defined, 28
and subordinating conjunctions in, 28

Compound predicates. *See* Predicates, combining sentences by joining

Compound sentences, 24–27
with *and*, *but*, or *or* in, 24, 26, 32
and commas used in, 24
defined, 24, 26

Compound subjects. *See* Subjects, combining sentences with

Conjunctions. See also *And*; *But*; *Or*
and commas used with, 24
coordinating, 24–27
defined, 24
subordinating, 28–31

Contractions, 104–107
apostrophes in, 104, 106, 184, 186
with *be*, 104, 184
defined, 104, 106, 184
with helping verbs (*has, have, had*), 104, 184
and homophones, 224, 226
with *I*, 184
list of, 104, 184
with *not*, 104, 148
with pronouns, 184–187, 224–227
with *will*, 104, 184

Coordinating Conjunctions, 24–27

D

Days
abbreviations of, 200
capitalization of, 196
and commas between days and years, 216

Declarative sentences
defined, 8, 10
and periods in, 8, 192

Demonstrative adjectives, 120–123
defined, 120
and nouns with, 120

Double negatives
defined, 148, 150
rule for, 148, 150

E

Editing, 10, 26, 34, 42, 46, 50, 54, 66, 70, 74, 78, 82, 90, 98, 102, 106, 118, 122, 126, 130, 134, 142, 146, 150, 166, 174, 186, 194, 198, 202, 206, 210, 214, 218, 222, 226, 230

End punctuation. *See also* Punctuation, exclamation marks, periods, question marks in sentences, 8, 192, 194

Exclamation marks
in exclamations, 8, 192
in quotations, 220

Exclamatory sentences
defined, 8, 10
and exclamation marks, 8, 92
in quotations, 220

F

Formal/Informal, 147, 183, 187, 215, 223

Fragments, 32–35
correcting, 32
defined, 32, 34

Friendly letters, 216, 218. *See also* Letters
capitalization in, 216
commas in, 216, 218
defined, 216
parts of, 216

Future tense, 76–79
defined, 76, 78
with *will*, 76, 78

G

Good. *See also* Adjectives, *good* and *bad* as; Adverbs, *well* vs. *good*
in comparisons, 132–137

Greetings. *See* Letters, capitalization in, colons in, commas in, parts of

H

Has, have, had
in contractions, 104, 184
as helping verbs, 84, 88, 90
and irregular verbs used with, 96, 98, 100, 102
with main verb, 88
and subject-verb agreement, 88, 90
and tenses of, 88, 96, 98, 100, 102

He, she, it. *See* Agreement, pronoun-verb

Headings. *See* Letters, parts of

Helping verbs, 84–87, 88–91. See also *Has, have, had*
be as, 84
in contractions, 104, 184
defined, 84, 86
and main verbs used with, 84, 88
and subject-verb agreement, 88, 90
and tenses of, 88, 96, 98, 100, 102
will as, 84

Holidays, capitalization of, 196

Homophones, 224–227
defined, 224

I

I, 172–175. *See also* Agreement, pronoun-verb; Subject pronouns
in contractions, 184

Imperative sentences
defined, 8, 10
and periods in, 8, 192

Informal/formal. *See* Formal/Informal

Informative/Explanatory texts, 199

Initials
as abbreviations, 200
and capitalization of, 200
defined, 200

Inside address. *See* Letters, parts of

Interrogative sentences
defined, 8, 10
and question marks in, 8, 192
in quotations, 220

Introductory words
and commas, use of, 212, 214

Irregular plural nouns, 48–51
defined, 48, 50

Irregular verbs, 96–99, 100–103
with helping verbs (*has, have, had*), 96, 98, 100, 102
spelling rules for, 96, 98, 100, 102

Italics
in titles, 204
and underlining, 204

Its, it's. *See* Homophones

L

Letters, 216–219
business, 216, 218
capitalization in, 216
colons in, 216, 218
commas in, 216, 218
friendly, 216, 218
parts of, 216, 218

Linking verbs, 80–83
be as, 80–83
defined, 80
with nouns, 80
and subjects with, 80, 82
and subject-verb agreement, 80, 82
and tenses of, 80

***-ly*, adverbs ending in**, 136

M

Magazines. *See* Capitalization, in titles; Italics, in titles

Main verbs, 84–87, 88
defined, 84
and helping verbs used with, 84, 88

***Me*, as object pronoun**, 172–175

Modals, 84–87

Months
abbreviations of, 200
capitalization of, 196

More*, *most
and spelling rules (with adjectives and adverbs), 128, 130, 140, 142

N

Names, capitalization of, 196

Narrative, 91, 135

Negatives, 148–151. *See also* Double negatives; *No*; *Not*
defined, 148
list of, 148

Newspapers. *See* Capitalization, in titles; Italics, in titles

No. *See also* Negatives
commas used with, 212, 214
in contractions, 148

Not. *See also* Negatives
in contractions, 104, 148

Nouns
abstract, 40–43
adjectives used with, 112, 114, 120, 144, 146
articles used with, 116, 118
combining sentences with, 47, 175
common, 40–43
defined, 40
with *good* and *well*, 144, 146
and irregular plurals, 48–51
plural, 44–47, 48–51, 52, 64, 66, 68, 70, 80, 88, 90, 120
possessive, 52–55
and possessive pronouns, 176, 178
in predicate of sentence, 47
in prepositional phrases, 152, 156
and pronouns, 160, 163, 171
proper, 40–43, 196–199
singular, 44–47, 48, 50, 52, 64, 66, 68, 70, 80, 88, 90, 116
and spelling rules for plurals, 44, 46, 48, 50
and spelling rules for possessives, 52
as subject of sentence, 64, 66, 68, 70
and subject pronouns, 64, 68, 80, 88, 90, 164–167, 175
and subject-verb agreement, 64, 66, 68, 70, 80, 82, 90

O

Object pronouns, 168–171. See also *Me*, as object pronoun
combining sentences, 175
defined, 168, 170
list of, 168
singulars and plurals of, 168

Online, 11, 15, 19, 23, 27, 31, 35, 43, 47, 51, 55, 63, 67, 71, 75, 79, 83, 87, 91, 95, 99, 103, 107, 115, 119, 123, 127, 131, 135, 139, 143, 147, 151, 155, 163, 167, 171, 175, 179, 183, 187, 195, 199, 203, 207, 211, 215, 219, 223, 227, 231

Opinion, 227

Or
to combine sentences with, 24, 26, 27, 47
in compound sentences, 24, 26, 27
as coordinating conjunction, 24–27

P

Past tense, 72–75, 76
defined, 72
with helping verbs, 88, 96, 98, 100, 102
with irregular verbs, 96, 98, 100, 102
and linking verbs, 80
and spelling rules for, 72, 74, 96, 98, 100, 102
and subject-verb agreement, 80

Periods
in abbreviations, 200, 202
in sentences, 8, 192

Plural nouns, 44–47, 48–51
with article *the*, 116
defined, 44
and demonstrative adjectives, 120
irregular forms, 48–51
with linking verbs, 80
spelling of, 44, 46, 48, 50, 52
as subjects, 64, 66, 68, 70
verb agreement with, 64, 66, 68, 70, 80, 88, 90

Plural pronouns, 160, 168
as objects, 168
as subjects, 160
and verb agreement with, 64, 68, 80, 88, 90, 164–167

Poems, and quotation marks, 204

Possessive nouns, 52–55
and apostrophes in, 52
defined, 52, 54
and possessive pronouns, 176
singulars and plurals of, 52
spelling rules for, 52

Possessive pronouns, 176–179
and contractions, 224, 226
defined, 176
and homophones, 224, 226
list of, 176, 178
and nouns used with, 176, 178

Predicates. *See also* Verb tense
combining sentences by joining, 23
complete, 12, 14, 16, 20
defined, 12
in sentences, 12, 14, 16, 19, 20, 23, 24, 26, 32, 47, 60
simple, 20–23
and subjects with, 12, 16, 20, 47, 60
and verbs, 60, 62, 71

Prepositional phrases
defined, 152, 154
with nouns or pronouns 152, 154

Prepositions, 152–155
defined, 152
list of, 152

Present tense, 64–67, 68–71, 76
defined, 64
with helping verbs, 88
of irregular verbs, 96, 100
and linking verbs, 80
and pronoun-verb agreement, 166
spelling rules for, 64, 68, 164, 166
and subject-verb agreement, 64, 66, 68, 70, 80, 88, 95

Progressive forms of verbs, 92–95

Pronouns. *See also* Object pronouns; Subject pronouns
and antecedent agreement, 160–163
combining sentences with, 175
and contractions, 184–187, 224–227
and homophones, 224, 227
I and *me*, 172–175
and nouns, 160, 163
possessives, 176–179, 224, 226
in prepositional phrases, 152, 154
and pronoun-verb agreement, 64, 68, 80, 88, 90, 164–167
singulars and plurals of, 80, 160, 168
as subject of sentence, 64, 68, 80, 88, 90, 160–163, 164, 166, 172
you, 160

Pronoun-verb agreement. *See* Agreement, pronoun-verb

Proofreading Checklist, 11, 15, 31, 51, 55, 59, 63, 79, 83, 87, 91, 95, 99, 103, 107, 123, 127, 131, 135, 143, 147, 151, 167, 179, 187, 199, 203, 207, 215, 219, 223, 227, 231

Proper nouns, 40–43, 196–199
and capitalization of, 40, 42, 196, 198
defined, 40, 196

Punctuation. *See also* End punctuation
apostrophes, 52, 104, 106, 184, 186
colons, 216, 218
commas, 24, 208, 210, 212, 214, 216, 218, 220
exclamation marks, 8, 192, 220
in letters, 216, 218
periods, 8, 192, 200, 202
question marks, 8, 192, 220
quotation marks, 204, 220, 222

Q

Question marks
in interrogative sentences, 8, 192
in quotations, 220

Questions. *See* Interrogative sentences

Quotation marks
in quotations, 220, 222
with titles, 204

Quotations, 220–223
capitalization in, 220
commas in, 220
defined, 220
punctuation in, 220
quotation marks in, 220, 222

R

Relative adverbs, 180–183

Relative pronouns, 180–183

Revising Sentences, 35, 43, 67, 75, 107, 119, 139, 151, 155, 163, 171, 195

Run-on sentences, 32–35, 192
correcting, 32
defined, 32, 34

S

Sentence completion, 14, 18, 22, 30, 62, 86, 94, 114, 138, 154, 162, 170, 178, 182

Sentences. *See also* Combining Sentences; Revising Sentences; Write Your Own
capital letters in, 8, 192, 194
combining, 19, 23, 24, 26, 47, 71, 163, 175, 211
combining with adjectives, 115
and commas in, 24, 212, 214
compound, 24–27, 32
with conjunctions, 24, 26, 47
declarative, 8, 10, 192, 220
defined, 8, 12, 60
and end punctuation in, 8, 192, 194
exclamatory, 8, 10, 192, 220
fragments, 32–35
imperative, 8, 10, 192, 220
interrogative, 8, 10, 192, 220
and nouns in, 43, 47
and predicates in, 12, 14, 16, 19, 20, 23, 24, 26, 32, 47, 60
and pronouns in, 160, 164, 171, 172, 174
pronoun-verb agreement in, 164–167
and punctuation in, 8, 192, 220
and quotations, 220
and run-ons, 32–35, 192
and series in, 208, 211
simple, 24, 26
and subjects in, 12, 14, 16, 19, 20, 23, 24, 26, 32, 47, 60, 64, 66, 68, 70, 80, 82, 84, 172, 174, 175
and subject-verb agreement in, 64, 66, 68, 70, 80, 82, 88, 90
and verbs in, 60, 64, 66, 68, 70, 80, 82

Series, 208–211
and commas used in, 208–211
defined, 208

Simple predicates, 20–23
and complete predicates, 20, 22
defined, 20

Simple sentences, defined, 12, 24, 26

Simple subjects, 16–19
and complete subjects, 16, 18
defined, 16

Simple tenses, 76

Singular nouns, 44–47, 48, 50
with *a*, *an*, *the*, 116, 118
defined, 44
and demonstrative adjectives, 120

with linking verbs, 80
and spelling of irregular plurals, 48, 50
as subjects, 64, 66, 68, 70
verb agreement with, 64, 66, 68, 70, 80, 88, 90

Singular pronouns, 160, 163
as objects, 168
as subjects, 164
and verb agreement, 80

Songs, quotation marks, used with, 204

Spelling
of adverbs, 136, 140, 142. See also *More, most*
in comparisons, 124, 126, 128, 130, 140, 142
of contractions, 104, 106
and dictionary use for, 15, 31, 91, 95, 135, 224, 228
of homophones, 224–227
of irregular plural nouns, 48, 50
of irregular verbs, 96, 98, 100, 102
of plural nouns, 44, 46
of possessive nouns, 52
in pronoun-verb agreement, 164, 166
in subject-verb agreement, 64, 68, 88
and verb tenses, 64, 72, 88, 96, 98, 100, 102, 164, 166

Statements. *See* Declarative sentences

State names, 200

Subject pronouns, 160–163, 172, 174
combining sentences with, 163, 175
defined, 160, 162
I as, 160, 172–175
and pronoun-verb agreement, 64, 68, 80, 88, 90, 164–167
singulars and plurals of, 164

Subjects
combining sentences with, 19, 175
complete, 12, 14, 16, 18, 20
defined, 12
and helping verbs, 88
I as, 160, 172–175
and linking verbs, 80, 82
pronouns as, 64, 68, 80, 88, 160–163, 164, 166, 172, 174, 175
and pronoun-verb agreement, 64, 68, 80, 88, 90, 164–167
in sentences, 12, 14, 16, 19, 20, 23, 24, 26, 32, 47, 60, 64, 66, 68, 70, 80, 82, 160, 175
simple, 16–19
and subject-verb agreement, 64, 66, 68, 70, 80, 82, 88, 90
and verbs, 60, 80, 82

Subject-verb agreement. *See* Agreement, subject-verb

Subordinating conjunctions, 28–31

T

Tense. *See* Verb tense

The. See *A, an, the*

They're, their, there. *See* Homophones

This, that, these, those. *See* Demonstrative adjectives

Titles. See also *A, an, the*, in titles; Capitalization, in titles; Italics, in titles
capitalization in, 196, 198, 204, 206
and quotation marks used with, 204
of songs and poems, 204

U

Underlining. *See* Italics, and underlining

V

Verbs. *See also* Verb tense
action, 60–63, 64, 164, 166, 168, 170, 171, 172, 174
and adverbs, 136, 138, 144, 146
combining sentences with, 71
and contractions, 104, 184, 226
defined, 60, 62
helping, 84–87, 88–91
irregular, 96–99, 100–103
linking, 80–83
main, 84–87, 88
and object pronouns, 168, 170, 171, 172
as predicates in sentences, 60, 62, 71
and pronoun-verb agreement, 64, 68, 80, 88, 90, 164–167
in sentences, 60, 64, 66, 68, 70, 80, 82
spelling rules for, 64, 68, 72, 74, 88, 96, 98, 100, 102, 164, 166
and subjects, 60, 80, 82
and subject-verb agreement, 64, 66, 68, 70, 80, 82, 88, 90

Verb tense
defined, 64
future, 76–79
with helping verbs (*has, have, had*), 88, 96, 98, 100, 102
with irregular verbs, 96, 98, 100, 102
with linking verb *be*, 80–83
past, 72–75, 76, 80, 88, 96, 98, 100, 102
and predicates, 60, 62, 71
present, 64–67, 68–71, 76, 80, 88, 96, 100
and pronoun-verb agreement with, 64, 68, 80, 88, 164–167
simple tenses, 76
spelling rules for, 64, 68, 72, 74, 88, 100, 102, 164, 166
and subject-verb agreement with, 64, 66, 68, 70, 80, 82, 88, 90
and *will* used in future tense, 76, 78

W

We, you, they. See Agreement, pronoun-verb

Well. See Adverbs, *well* vs. *good*

Will
in contractions, 104, 184
in future-tense verbs, 76, 78
as helping verb, 84

Words often confused, 228–231

Words often misspelled, 224–227

Worse, worst. *See* Adjectives, *good* and *bad* as

Write Your Own, 11, 15, 31, 51, 55, 63, 79, 83, 87, 91, 95, 99, 103, 123, 127, 131, 135, 143, 147, 167, 179, 187, 199, 203, 207, 215, 219, 223, 227

Y

Years, comma between day and year, 216

***Yes*, commas used with**, 212, 214

***You*, as subject pronoun**, 160

You're, your. *See* Homophones